Succession Planning for the Family Owned Business: A Blueprint for the Future

by *Mike Fager and Dave McKinney*

To Kyle Fager

Without your tireless literary and editorial efforts,
this book would not have been possible

Foreword

There are only two things that can happen to your business. Either it succeeds or it fails.

If your fortune is the former, the expert critics who like to frequent your local coffee shop will say that your business succeeded only because you are a lucky son of a gun. If your fortune is the latter, these same critics will claim that your business failed because you're a dumb son of a gun.

Either way, you're a son of a gun.

But all kidding aside, let's talk about the reality of the situation. What the experts at the coffee shop don't realize is that running a business is very much like pole vaulting. It's an awful lot harder than it looks. It has required the focused application of your time, talent, temperament, and total dedication to succeed. If I may enter a mixed metaphor, the wolves have always been at the back door and yet you've always managed to avoid them. Maybe you pole vaulted over them.

The bottom line is that you are a successful small business owner. As such, it can be stated that you have survived this long on the back of grit and determination – and, yes, you were indeed the recipient of a little luck, here and there. Other members of your family and, of course, your employees have perhaps been a big help, as well.

Now that all that time and trouble is wrapping up, you may feel like you're coming to a crossroads in your life. Crossroads or no, *something* (other than the flashy cover, of course) prompted you to pick up this book. As the great New York Yankee philosopher Yogi Berra once said, "If you come to a fork in the road, take it." It may seem absurd, but we couldn't have put it any better. At the heart of this rather cryptic advice is a strong and true message: When you reach a crossroads, it's time to take action. Develop a plan. Communicate that plan to your family. And take action.

Procrastination, after all, is very rarely a good thing. The long term success of your business and your family may well be at stake, after all.

The book that you are now holding represents a long and sometimes arduous effort to solidify an extremely complex topic as succinctly as possible. Obviously, in undertaking such a vast subject, we must admit that, here and there, the owner of a family business is likely to encounter problems that are not addressed herein. As always, it is best to contact a trusted financial or legal professional when such situations arise.

Of course we cannot summarize the writing process of this book without offering special thanks to George Abraham of BES Appraisals. The appraisals chapter would have been forever stuck on the drawing board if not for his insight and expertise. Special thanks should also be extended to Kelly Epperson. Her expert tax knowledge as well as her sharp editorial eye greatly improved many of these pages.

So in closing, we hope that you find this book of value. We hope it helps you "take that fork in the road" and accomplish all your major goals for retirement and business succession. Good luck and good planning.

Mike Fager and Dave McKinney

TABLE OF CONTENTS

Section 1:
Introduction

Chapter 1

Begin the Planning Process Now; He Who Hesitates Is Lost

Point of fact: Most family businesses fail to navigate the rough passage across generational tides. Without proper planning, the business that you and your family have worked so hard to bring afloat may wind up losing direction and crashing on the rocks of inability or carelessness when passed to future generations.

How do you know if you've planned properly for the future of your business? Ask yourself this question: "Have I spent more time planning family vacations than I have on planning the transition of my business?" If the answer to this question is "yes," then your business is either vastly unprepared for the future or you enjoy some extraordinarily well-run vacations.

"So You're Involved in a Family Owned Business." Upon perusing its chapters, you might think that this title – though remarkably cheesy – could have been considered for the book that you are now holding. Simplicity, they say, is often the most effective hook. While it is true that within these pages, you will find no centerfold spread or snapshots of celebrities' babies, the subject matter, to the small business owner, will hopefully be every bit as riveting.

Although some of our chapters carry spellbinding titles such as "Estate Planning Issues" and "Financing the Transition" and, as a result, would seem rather broad – perhaps a book in themselves – what you will find is that they are all specifically geared toward several topics commonly associated with family owned businesses.

But since there are clearly many concepts that would seem more pertinent to the owner of such a business, the question then becomes, "Why focus on succession planning now?" It's an honest question – and one that you should ask before it's too late.

The answer is simple: *He who hesitates is lost.* The reason we've taken the time to sit down and pen this book that purposely addresses succession planning for the family owned business is that it is *absolutely essential.*

We realize that planning for the future of your business can seem a rather heroic task, especially when faced with all of the short-term problems that most small businesses must endure. In response, we kick off this chapter by addressing all of the reasons to *not* begin the planning process now.

Reasons *Not* to Begin the Planning Process Now

1. *Things are going exceedingly well – "The Good Times Will Never Change" Complex*

It is easy to get sucked into the trap. The "good times will never end complex" might sneak up on you without you even noticing. From about the time we hit puberty, when met with success, the human tendency is to adopt the pathos of almost euphoric infallibility. Oftentimes, we are perhaps less reverent of potential failure than we should be. Especially when disaster – and, as a result, failure – can strike at any time, usually without warning.

"The good times will never change!" Unless your business is called "The Land of Oz," you must realize that this career

Candyland does not exist. Nothing is perfect. At least, nothing stays perfect.

Even those of us who do maintain an appropriate level of career-related paranoia may not realize the importance of planning for the future. Many times in a successful business, the pressure of "how do I maintain this success while I'm alive?" often clouds the more significant issue of "how do I ensure that this success continues after I'm gone?"

It is important to note that these are separate issues and that this dichotomy is absolute. There is no such thing as a business that can pass without proper planning and preparation from generation to generation without tribulation, without disagreement, and without fail.

We realize when things are going exceedingly well it's difficult to imagine a time when the opposite is true. But if you wish to watch your successful business pass safely to your children and then your children's children, you must bite the bullet and overcome these common biases. You must prepare for a successful succession. It does not happen magically.

2. *It's difficult to play a good fiddle when Rome is burning at your desk*

There are always 43 other problems reaching up over your desk to devour you. Gruesome, yes – but almost always true. You know what it's like to operate a family business or you wouldn't be reading this book. It's difficult. Everyday, you are met with new challenges and – because there just aren't enough hours in a day – these challenges tend to stockpile and a sense of urgency begins to take over.

We realize that your 43 problems are more easily addressed than succession planning. The topic itself may seem morbid or unpleasant, if not just entirely difficult. Ensuring the future success of your business is oftentimes far more trying than the many challenges waiting on your desk.

The most common cause for the absence of succession planning can be accounted for fairly simply: we tend to do the urgent and the easy long before we even think about the important. It is completely normal to feel just-too-busy to plan for the future. "Just-too-busy," however, is just a state of mind, one that can be easily overcome. Take a step back and think about what is most important to you in life. If "getting caught up at work" is your answer, then perhaps this book isn't for you. If "leaving the legacy of a successful business behind – one that will help my family maintain a comfortable lifestyle for many generations to come" is your answer, then you owe it to yourself to put your 43 problems aside and take the time to build a detailed succession plan.

3. *"Of course I will live forever and always be of sound mind and body."*

Nobody wants to think about death or disability. They're humbling issues – and who wants to be humbled? In response to this common reaction, people tend to do something very silly: they develop a subconscious sense – or, rather, a denial of reality – that they are somehow above their own mortality.

Yet the fact remains that the potential for death or disability bears some small part in everyday life. Because disaster could strike at any time, you owe it to yourself to look past the discomfort associated with addressing your own vulnerability and take the steps necessary to ensure that those who love you are cared for and well directed in the event that they suddenly need to fill your shoes as leader of the family business.

4. *"What will happen to my key employees after I'm gone?"*

During the tenure of your leadership, it is likely that you have developed strong relationships with many of your employees. It is equally likely that, without several key employees, your business would not have met such wonderful success. If this is true, you have probably pondered the following questions. If not, let's ponder together: What if some of these employees are members of your family? Should they be entitled to all or part of the control of your company once you are ready to pass the torch? Will the new owner treat them fairly and with as much respect as you have over the years? Will their job status be unaffected?

We recognize that most business owners who begin to think about transition planning recognize these issues and find reason to worry. Oftentimes, this worry is enough to make most people ignore planning altogether. What is remarkable about this common reaction is that it is precisely the opposite of what it should be. The only way to ensure that your key employees keep their jobs and are treated fairly is to outline an employee-relations-conscious succession plan.

5. *"If I sell my business, what'll I do next?"*

If you own a successful family business, odds are that somewhere along the line you have been dubbed with the affectionate moniker of "the workaholic." Retirement, for you, can seem to be the most stressful of concepts to bear. Of course, there is a great deal of uncertainty associated with retirement. It is an excellent and important question to ask: what *will* you do next?

And, if you have somehow managed to overcome this most traumatic of hurdles – perhaps you have a company psychiatrist who keeps you well-medicated – you still have to wonder whether or not the proceeds garnered from the sale of your business will be sufficient to keep your head above financial waters for the rest of your life. Will you be able to maintain the lifestyle to which you have grown accustomed?

Most people react to these anxieties by assuming that they will be able to maintain quality leadership throughout their lives. And, even if this isn't the case, they recognize that, without having a job to do everyday, they may go quietly but completely mad. So who needs retirement?

Unless you are one of those fortunate few who were constructed out of invulnerable metal, you need retirement. The aging process affects us all. Sometimes, it can wear on your ability to lead and make appropriate business decisions. If not for the sake of yourself, then for the sake of your family – plan appropriately for retirement. If not for the sake of your family, then for the sake of your business and its leadership – plan appropriately for retirement.

Plans are more flexible than you may think. You may be able to draft a plan that allows you to maintain a great deal of control of your business without all the hassle of complex decision making. Plus, it is possible to continue earning a living through your more passive role and therefore avoid the dreaded "fixed income." Think of this kind of transition plan as a vehicle that allows you to pass from leader to mentor. You may be surprised by how fulfilling the latter role can be.

6.   *"Will I choke on the tax bill?"*

Without appropriate planning and a sophisticated approach to asset protection, the answer to this question is most assuredly "yes." But, as we have already discussed, planning is often a trying matter. This, coupled with the fear of the great tax meltdown, is usually enough to keep most owners of a family business from addressing these issues until it's too late.

This is understandable. It is, after all, a well-founded concern. "Why should I have to pay so much money for selling something so dear to me?" An excellent question, but a misappropriated one.

Perhaps you *don't* have to pay a great deal of money for selling the business that you have worked so hard to build. A proper family transition plan – one that is littered with well-advised tax reduction strategies – can help you and your family avoid often crippling tax liabilities.

7. *"Can my successor run the business as effectively as I have?"*

This is difficult to say and almost impossible to predict. You, after all, are the one who built the business from the ground up. You're talented. There is almost no way of knowing whether or not your successor can handle things quite like you can.

Since you are involved in a family business, we can throw another intriguing problem into the mix. Who will be your successor? A son? Daughter? A son- or daughter-in-law? A combination of these? How do you pass the business on to one of them without fear of angering the others?

And if we can make the assumption that you are planning on passing the business to a family member, is there any way to really know whether this family member is even interested in taking over for you? When dealing with family and the complex emotions associated with family, this is a difficult question both to ask and to answer.

The answer to many of these questions is – you guessed it – "be sure to plan properly for the future." You cannot assume anything. Meet with your family, especially those who are the best candidates to serve as your successor. Talk about your retirement and the prospect of keeping the business within the family.

The most critical days for any business are the earliest days. The best thing that you can do for your business is to ensure that those days go as smoothly as possible. Your successor, after all, cannot be expected to run things as effectively as you have if he/she has to worry about tax liability or debt issues.

Now that all of the reasons to avoid succession planning have been effectively shot down, we can move on to a sensible list of reasons to begin the planning process now.

Reasons to Begin the Planning Process Now

1. *The Most Important Problem On Your Desk*

As previously discussed, you are daily faced with many problems to deal with. Urgency – as it is with most people – may very well be your driving force.

Perhaps your sense of urgency is so high that you've decided to skip the last four pages in order to save time. If so, then you have missed out on plenty of subliminal messages that indicate the aforementioned reasons *not* to begin the planning process now actually double as reasons *to* begin the planning process now. We're sneaky – we know.

Upon reading the seven reasons not to begin succession planning, you should have begun to build a sense that, though it may seem tedious or even dreadful, succession planning is *the* most important problem on your desk. And if your sense of urgency is your only driving force, let us now make this statement: Planning for the future of your business may be more urgent than you think.

2. *Things Change*

Let's put the most disturbing foot forward, shall we? Key personnel – including you, your top employees, and your potential successors – die, become disabled, divorced, disinterested, or disgruntled for myriad reasons. Considering these factors – and their potential to arrive suddenly and without warning – it is easy to see that change can be a most daunting factor to consider. And *no* business is invulnerable to change.

Even the greatest success has a tendency to turn. Chalk this one up to the chaos factor. Even if you are at the top of your game, your business is dominating all of its competition, and profits are at their highest and increasing every quarter, you run the risk of failure. Consumer interest fluctuates violently and markets tend to shift.

Consider this: the value of your business stands the chance of actually decreasing over time. Plenty of things could change to bring this about. For example, in the coming years, you could make some key decisions that wind up altering the direction and, as a result, the growth of your company in the long run – and, to quote the old saying, "If you're not growing, you're dying." Directly competing businesses may meet with greater success which further devalues your business. The demand for your products or services may decline or even disappear. The list goes on.

Whenever a business finds success, the most enterprising entrepreneurs tend to notice. New competition always seems to crop up at the most inopportune times. This, of course, requires increased effort on your part to stave off this new competition and thus maintain the success and value of your business. But even the most visionary of leaders can't win all the time. Sometimes, the competition can run you straight out of the market.

3.   The Lethargy Principle

This subject, in a way, caters to the idea that nobody can outlast the effects of time. Aging brings a whole range of new problems to deal with. These problems have a tendency to permeate both personal and professional life – and can really slight a person's effectiveness as a small business owner. Aging, too, can be the most grievous of problems because it is often ignored or denied. Most people are too proud to admit that they lack the ability or desire to complete the tasks that they once handled with ease.

People get tired. Maybe you can't quite lead 'em like you used to. Maybe the weariness creeps up on you much earlier in the day. Maybe you lack the energy or desire to meet all of the demands of owning and operating a family business – and, as a result, key problems go overlooked and your business stumbles, falters, and slows down. Obviously, this can greatly affect the success of your business and its chance of surviving through the next generation.

People get bored. Having responsibility for the same tasks for decades can get rather tedious. Even workaholics get bored eventually. The older we get, the closer we come to having "seen it all" – and with this concept comes a distinct lack of interest. If we've seen it all, then how can anything surprise or challenge us? Boredom has a tendency to wear on even the most solid of businesses. You and your successors must be capable of recognizing and alleviating the problem before it's too late.

When a company's leader is bored or tired, the most demanding problems seem to magnify. Fighting fierce competition and dealing with economic downturns begin to look like insurmountable tasks. The moment you realize that you'd rather see your business slump than put forth the effort to combat your competition is the moment that control of your company should be passed to your established successor.

4. The Spouse Factor

Family businesses have several complexities not found in most other small firms. Family is personal, business is professional – and family owned businesses, oftentimes, cannot help but mix the two influences.

One of the more significant of these personal/professional complexities is what we call "the spouse factor." Whether he/she is directly involved in your company – like it or not – your spouse has at least a minor influence on many of your professional decisions. There is nothing wrong with this. It is both normal and healthy to confide in your spouse and desire to include him/her in what amounts to be some of your most important choices in life.

The spouse factor, however, has the potential to carry two harmful influences:

The first is that your husband/wife might not be as agreeable to your working-till-death plan as you are. Even though you have never planned to retire, your spouse may have a different notion of what "the golden years" should bring. He/she may have his/her heart set on those six months a year in Florida and be completely oblivious to the idea that you have no intention of ever hanging up your spurs. This discrepancy has the potential to lead to a conflict of almost epic proportions – which could cause you to lose your job quickly and under uncertain terms, your spouse to give up his/her dream of retiring to a tropical climate, or your marriage to end.

This brings us to the second harmful influence: Divorce. Divorce enjoys an alarmingly powerful presence within our culture. It has come to the point where failing to pre-plan for divorce seems idiotic or naïve at best. Without proper planning, the effects of a rocky divorce on a family owned business can be nothing short of tempestuous.

5.   *Falling Behind*

Most successful family businesses took many years to build. In the time it took to bring your business to where it is today, how much has changed? Think of the drastic upswing of economic development. Think of the evolution of our culture and society. Think of the ever-encroaching legal world. Have you kept up?

This is surely a troubling question. And all of this disregards perhaps the most significant issue that threatens the health of your business: technology. Whether you own a product- or service-based business, all or parts of your company stand the chance of being rendered obsolete by new technology. The process may have already begun without you even noticing. If this is the case, it may be time to pass the family business on to a younger generation – whose leadership will likely bring a broader understanding of new technology and the ever-changing marketplace.

If you haven't already, perhaps you will soon be reaching the "top of your game." The fact is that every business comes to a point where, without a great deal of effort, it will no longer improve in any significant fashion. This is called the plateau effect – and overcoming it may require more effort than you are willing to put forth.

Besides, if you have reached this "top of your game" state, it is likely that your business is running more smoothly and is worth far more than it has ever been in the past. At this point, it would obviously be an excellent time for you to sell off your interests. But what about your successor? If you intend to keep the business within the family for generations to come, wouldn't it be in your best interest to sell the business to your successor when it is a little more affordable? Not necessarily. With higher price comes higher value – and if your successor inherits the company when it is at its strongest, although he/she may have paid a great deal for it, he/she may find it easier to garner a significant return. Certainly, if the business is at its strongest, the transition will be easier for the new leader to handle.

6. A Lifetime of Risk

Owning and operating your own business for the majority of your life is a highly risky way to live. Over time, people's tolerance for such risk tends to wane, making every business endeavor seem treacherous. Unfortunately, risk is an inseparable part of business. Those who are incapable of tolerating it are unfit to lead.

The question often arises, "How much longer will this business be profitable?" It is a question that everyone must ask – not for the sake of their pocketbooks but for the sake of their children. If you feel that your company's profitability days are numbered, then you must ponder two notions: Either you need to take steps to ensure a broader sense of long-term success for your business and then draft your succession plan or your risk tolerance has declined of late and you should perhaps "get out before it's too late."

7. Success and *Failure as a Reason to Leave*

If your company enjoys a great deal of success:

There will come a time when one of your professional advisors clues you in to the notion that your business has reached its peak value. Peak value is good for two reasons. We have already discussed these reasons in brief. First, if you want to make your millions, selling at peak value is an excellent time to do so. And second, if you want to ensure your successor's success, do so by allowing them to take over your business when it is booming rather than crashing.

If your company is unsuccessful of late:

Begin by ignoring everything that was written in the above paragraph. Of course, no one wants to dump a failing load on a family member. Before you decide to pass things on to the next generation, you must properly assess whether your business is failing because of its declining relationship to the marketplace or because it is in dire need of a fresh mind to lead it. You must also assess your successor's tolerance for risk. He/she may be completely comfortable with – not to mention capable of – turning your business completely around.

~~~

So far, we have shed light on seven reasons *not* and seven reasons *to* begin the planning process now – notice the intricate balance – all of them leading to the same essential point: If you don't have a succession plan in place, you'd better get cracking. From here – as most well-crafted introductory chapters do – we will move on to summarize what to expect from the chapters to come.

The Six Dangerous "D's"

The "Dangerous D's" include death, divorce, disability, disagreement, disaster, and depression. All of the more uplifting notions, we're afraid, will have to be confined to later chapters.

The goal of this chapter, if properly executed, is to further shock you into submission and generally pound home the idea that your family business cannot survive without a well-documented and well-thought-out buy/sell agreement. You will never again question "Why in the world do I need to think about succession planning?"

Estate Planning Issues

Don't let the overly-simplistic title fool you – this chapter is a must read for anyone who wants to maintain as much control over their assets as possible. Within these pages, you will learn how to save on taxes, manage your insurance, and pass your estate to your heirs the way *you* want to.

Of course, if you haven't thought much about your own estate planning issues, there is much documentation in your future – but it is important to follow through. There are, after all, many steps and strategies to pursue in order to maintain a stable and controllable estate.

Family Communications

Everyone knows that maintaining harmony within a family is often a trying if not impossible task. Things are complicated further for those families that own interest in a business.

This chapter explains that, even if things sometimes get heated, simply opening the lines of communication with your family can often smooth out the transition process. Without family communication, it is impossible to predict or even understand your company's potential for a successful future.

Asset Protection

In today's world, protecting oneself from financial predators is vital. This chapter details who should be concerned about asset protection, outlines a series of tried-and-true strategies for protecting your assets from legal harm, and lists steps to take when selecting the strategy that's right for you.

Strategies include investment oriented insurance products, offshore investing, asset protection trusts, exemption planning, using the corporate shield, and applying good old fashioned common sense. Any one or a combination of these methods can be applied to protect oneself from harmful litigation. Make yourself immune to lawyers, creditors, and again, save on taxes.

Selecting Your Successor

In order to ensure the future success of your company, obviously, you must ensure that your successors are competent and capable of leading every bit as effectively as you have over the years. This chapter sheds light on some of the tools and tricks-of-the-trade to employ when evaluating and training your eventual successor.

We discuss the importance of first evaluating the desire of your successor to take over – you can't always assume that your son or daughter wants to follow in your footsteps. Once you've found an interested family member, you must assess their strengths and weaknesses. Then through your intent tutelage, you can help them hone their skills gradually in a comfortable setting. With proper training, your successors will have the advantage to keep your business on track and sailing successfully into the future.

Retaining Key Employees

Your successor, unfortunately, will not hold all of the same opinions and insights that you do. He/she may not see the value of various key employees that helped to make your company what it is today. Concurrently, you cannot expect all of your key employees to work as diligently or harmoniously with their new boss. Sometimes personalities clash.

In this section, we explain what it takes to ensure that your key employees keep their jobs and that your successor knows exactly how to manage them.

What's Your Business Really Worth – And Why Should You Care?

This chapter is all about sizing up your business. So why *should* you care? Because "the first day you think about selling your business is the first day you start it." It is important that you know what your company is worth when you pass it on to your children or other successors. For one thing, having your business properly appraised will ensure that you're getting a fair price from the buyer(s).

Many people don't even know who to turn to when seeking a business appraisal and, oftentimes, rely on their accountants or banks to complete the task. As you will see, this is just about the last thing one should do. This chapter discusses the most common complications associated with business appraisal and highlights seven different ways to informally evaluate your own firm.

Enhancing Value for the New Buyer

Obviously, whenever we prepare to sell something, we do everything we can to make it seem the most appealing. When we prepare to sell a car, we get it washed, touch up the paint, and tune up the engine. When we prepare to sell a house, we fix the leaky toilet, paint the walls, and clean out the closets. A business should be no different.

Enhancing value for the new buyer includes assessing a business' strengths and weaknesses, dropping potentially failing product or service lines, sizing yourself up to the competition, and doing everything you can to show profit before the sale.

Obviously, if you intend to pass the company on to a loved one, you have to be sure that things are in top working order.

Otherwise, you leave an unclean and potentially malfunctioning business to your less experienced heirs.

Financing the Transition

Every major life change seems to require a great deal of money. In this chapter, we outline several money-gathering strategies that you may not have considered. Employee Stock Ownership Plans (or ESOPs) can be a relatively painless – and highly effective – way to gradually pass your business on to your successors. In addition to easing the passage of a business from one owner to the next, an ESOP is appealing for several reasons which include a wide range of tax incentives created by Congress, the potential to create a slightly more motivated workforce, and the improvement of corporate debt capacity.

An ESOP can make passing the baton to the next generation a much smoother process. If you eventually plan to retire, look into an ESOP ASAP.

Tax Strategies and Charitable Planning

This chapter explains several key tax strategies to help alleviate some of the financial burden associated with the often devastating taxation of a businesses in transition. If the IRS scares you – and believe us, we're with you on that one – then this chapter is well worth a look.

You may be wondering about charitable giving. Even if you lack the desire to give back to a community that has given so much to you and your business, there are a great number of positives associated with charitable giving. A structured approach to the task can help you avoid some taxes and even keep your family business successful for many years to come.

Remember, You Sold It...Or Did You?

Retirement can be a stressful concept to consider. We offer suggestions on how to maintain some involvement in the family business, if that is what you choose, as well as how to transition gracefully into full-time retirement. For the majority of your life, you've been directing your family business. It's hard to imagine doing anything else. With this chapter, we'll help you expand your imagination to see the world of possibilities that lie before you now as you embark on the next phase of your life.

Remember, retirement isn't the end of life. It is the beginning of a new adventure.

~~~

Our goal with this initial chapter has been to explain the dire need for succession planning for the family owned business – that "He Who Hesitates Is Lost." Now that you agree, let's move on and delve into the finer points of the succession planning process.

Section 2:
Maintaining Your Business through Future Generations

Chapter 2

The Six Dangerous D's

One unfortunate aspect that makes operating a family owned business so unique is that there are several risk-factors to consider that would not even count as blips on the radar for businesses that do not depend upon one specific family for leadership. We have narrowed these risk-factors down to a group that will be known as the six "Dangerous D's." What makes them so dangerous is that, despite the fact that they are inevitable, they are often overlooked.

Before we begin with the Dangerous D's, we have an anecdotal story we would like to share.

Back in 1957, in rural northern Illinois, Brown Brothers Trucking, owned and operated by Tom and Harold Brown, enjoyed a steady stream of business and seemed poised for continued success. Each day, the brothers drove their trucks on basic milk routes, picking up their shipments by the barrel-load. They worked long days; their only break coming at lunch, where they would sit in the cabs of their trucks, drink raw milk, and eat the lunches that their wives had carefully packed for them each morning.

Those were the days when almost every farm in America had livestock and the service provided by Brown Brothers Trucking was in constant demand from the many farms in the area. The two brothers, indeed, had the respect and support of their community. Hopes were high and everything seemed as stable as could be.

Brown Brothers Trucking had several weaknesses that no one had considered, however. The first weakness – in keeping with our book's theme – was that they had not discussed any kind of succession plan or buy/sell agreement, however informal. The second was that Brown Brothers Trucking, like the town that supported it, was very small. In fact, the company consisted of only two trucks and two employees: the Brown brothers themselves. Which brings us to their final weakness: they were two equal owners with no outside employees.

By the end of 1957, Brown Brothers Trucking was essentially gone. In that year, Harold contracted leukemia – dying just two weeks after being diagnosed.

Since the brothers had never discussed a succession plan, and since the company had no interested parties outside the family, the company was left in the control of the surviving brother, Tom. Tom was left with several personal and professional problems. First, what percentage of the company was he now entitled to? Second, how was he to compensate his brother's wife for her loss? And, finally, how could he expect the company to continue without outside help?

Due to the medical and funeral costs of his brother – to say nothing of the paperwork it takes to transfer ownership of a family business – Tom could not afford to hire new help. The enterprise was small and not terribly profitable, after all. As such, Tom was forced to brave the remainder of the company's existence on his own.

Later in 1957, tragedy struck again when Tom contracted multiple sclerosis, rendering him completely incapable –

though he tried valiantly for many months – of running his portion of the truck route.

The company would not be able to make enough profits for the owner to sustain a steady and comfortable income while adequately paying two employees to take over the truck routes, especially considering the fact that that owner would also be responsible for staggeringly large medical bills in the coming months and years. Brown Brothers Trucking was simply unable to continue. What's more, the company had no value other than forced sale prices of its trucks and equipment.

The tragedies that occurred in that year, coupled with the loss of an otherwise successful family business, were emotionally and financially devastating to both Harold's and Tom's immediate families for many years.

The Brown brothers and their families were victims of two of the six Dangerous D's – death and disability. The other four include divorce, disagreement, disaster, and depression. As you can see, all of them are emotionally and professionally destructive issues – and, most of the time, they are upon us without advanced warning.

Even though the potential for these traumas to strike your family and your business is very real, there is always good news. Each of these dangerous D's can be circumvented by a carefully planned buy/sell agreement. This chapter provides the six most important reasons that you should be considering your own buy/sell agreement even as you read.

Death

Of the six D's, death is perhaps the most obvious threat because it is the only one that promises to affect us all. Because it carries such a well-recognized presence, most people plan for death in at least some small way, such as drafting a will.

But is a simple will enough? In almost all cases where a family business is involved, the answer is most certainly "no."

Death *is* one of the more difficult occurrences to overcome – oftentimes, businesses never fully recover from the loss of an owner, successor, or key employee. The talents and insights of the lost individual are gone for good – causing a negative and long-lasting impact on any family owned business. Death, after all, has a tendency to be rather final.

Furthermore, death – as with all of the other dangerous D's – always seems to arrive at the most inopportune times. Whatever problematic issues that the business was dealing with before the death of the owner or key employee seem to be magnified during the mourning period. Accounts receivables, accounts payables, and all sales issues are greatly complicated by the additional leg- and paperwork associated with picking up the deceased party's slack and tying up all of the loose ends left behind. It's Murphy's Law, hard at work (essentially, whatever can go wrong, does go wrong).

Complicating the issue even further is the fact that most deceased parties leave behind a widowed spouse. Surviving spouses are a potentially negative factor for two reasons: he/she may have little or no interest or ability to help run the business; and he/she may become a pure financial drain without contributing one iota of effort to the cause. In other words, more often than not, surviving spouses expect to do little or no work for a large share of company profits.

If we look back to the Brown Brothers' story – and we deal purely in hypotheticals – it is easy to see that a surviving spouse can complicate things greatly. If Harold had managed to find a way to keep his company going, hiring capable employees and generating profits as though nothing had changed, he would have been faced with the issue of how to compensate his brother's wife, Darlene. What might have seemed fair to one party might not have with the other. Harold might have had to find a way to include Darlene – whose frail stature wasn't exactly conducive to lifting heavy milk containers or even driving a large truck – in the business in order to justify the loss of half his profits. Darlene perhaps could have run the books but, given the small and therefore uncomplicated nature of the company, would that have been enough to earn her keep?

Another option that Harold could have taken, should he have been so inclined, would have been to buy out Darlene's interest in the company, making himself full owner. This strategy certainly would have been the easiest way to maintain a living while still allowing for room to hire an outside employee to run the trucks. His company may have had to scale back production, reducing itself to running only one truck, but, by and large, Harold would have been able to continue making a fairly comfortable living. Unfortunately, this was not an option, as Harold and Tom had failed to take out life insurance policies on one another. When his brother died, Harold was left broke and incapable of purchasing the other half of his company.

Like Harold, we all understand that death can be a most troubling and complicated occurrence. To one degree or another, we've all experienced the pain that it can bring. Make no mistake; without preparation, *no* business is safe from this most devastating event.

Divorce

Everyone who lives in this country knows that divorce carries a strong presence. In today's world, half of all marriages end in divorce. The premarital legal costs and effort necessary to ensure that divorce doesn't tear you and your family business apart are miniscule compared to the potential legal costs in processing a rough marital split.

But money isn't the only issue. Divorce can affect a person in many different – and profoundly deep – ways. When embarking upon this difficult journey, there is much to think about – how to tell the kids, how to handle custody, why the divorce is necessary in the first place – and a cluttered mind is often less effective. Family businesses are usually greatly affected by divorce simply because the divorcee involved in running the business becomes thoroughly distracted. And this carries over to the rest of the company. Divorce, in an indirect but notable way, can cause productivity to suffer.

Then there are the emotional issues to consider. Divorce tends to amplify any ongoing emotional situation in a person's life and can be directly linked to another of our dangerous D's: depression. As we will see, depression can lead to a host of new problems; including poor decision-making, a decline in work ethic, and lack of desire to lead or care for the company's success. Depression can come on slowly and often goes undetected. In the event of a divorce, it is likely to appear in some form or another, however slight.

Things are especially painful when both parties of the divorce are involved in the family business. Suddenly, a spouse becomes an ex-spouse – and yet you still have to see him/her everyday at work.

You're a business owner. Imagine if your ex-spouse was still an employee of the business that you manage. Imagine having to pay him/her both a salary *and* child support. Imagine the anxiety. Heated or otherwise unpleasant discussions would become a part of everyday life – and tension like this often leads to poor decisions that could adversely affect the company's future success.

If this is the case with your business, there are two points that all interested parties must consider: How important is your ex-spouse to the company? And are both divorcees capable of working together in the future? Once you have answered these questions, you have two options: Either keep the ex-spouse on as an employee if he/she is vital to the success of your organization and try to figure out a way to maintain harmony throughout the workplace; or discuss the best and least costly, both financially and effectually speaking, way to elbow the ex-spouse out of the business.

Without proper planning before the marriage ended, and without a detailed buy/sell agreement, buying out the interest of an ex-spouse may be complex and extremely costly. Some family businesses have literally died within the courtroom – due entirely to the fact that participating in the legal process is either highly distracting or expensive.

Disability

Thinking back to our story about Brown Brothers Trucking, it can be stated that disability is among the most surprising and devastating of the dangerous D's. Left without a contingency plan, upon the death of his brother and the discovery of his own crippling disease, Harold was left to bravely attempt to continue his portion of the work, sometimes crawling from the truck to the pick-up site.

Eventually, multiple sclerosis proved to be too much for Harold to overcome. He spent the better part of his life confined to a wheelchair – and the business he had worked so hard to build effectively died along with his brother.

No one wants to think about the potential for disability, though it is a potential that we all share. It is difficult to imagine managing a business without a clean bill of health – and even tougher to picture ourselves condemned to such a vulnerable state. We would all like to think that, even in the face of disability, we would be capable of maintaining the lifestyle to which we've grown accustomed. *Our* business wouldn't suffer. *We* would persevere.

Unfortunately, life is not like an after school special on network television. No matter how brave we are or how strong our spirit, disability can have a lasting impact on the family business. More often than not, the business partner who becomes disabled is unwilling or unable to make the same quality of contribution to the business. In a way, when an important partner becomes disabled, so too does the business itself.

One aspect of disability that makes it one of the most difficult D's to cope with is that the disabled owner or partner usually has the desire – if not the right – to continue to receive an income. If he/she was integral to the founding and eventual success of the business, what kind of person would be willing to shut him/her out in the cold? Just because a person is suddenly unable to contribute doesn't mean that he/she should be penalized financially. Sometimes, however, we cannot always follow natural human empathy. Sometimes, the business may not yet have reached a level where it can continue to provide an income for a non-participating employee, leaving the other business owners with their hands tied.

Again, think of the Brown brothers.

Disability has the unfortunate tendency of halting any business at the proverbial crossroads. Interested partners either have to justify paying a disabled partner for nothing or buying out his/her interests, leaving him/her disabled, unable to work, and unemployed. Unless the steps to take in the event of disability have been laid out in advance, this can be an almost impossible-to-justify decision to make. The potential for conflict is enormous.

Disagreement

Speaking of conflict, let's move on to disagreement. While it is probably true that disagreements occur at the office everyday, family owned businesses often step it up to blockbuster-caliber disagreements.

Disagreement is a unique member of the dangerous D's in that it has its own special place intertwined with all of its counterparts. Death, divorce, disability, disaster, and depression are all very complicated issues. Most of the time, this complication is directly related to the fact that they all have the tendency to lead to passionate disagreement. Knowing this, you would think that everyone would expect to run into disagreement at some point or another in their careers as owners of their respective family businesses and therefore draft plans to deal with such situations, wouldn't you? We would. Although, truth be told, before we started doing research for this book project, we hadn't yet planned on how to handle business-ending disagreements. Don't tell anyone.

People can be very opinionated. So opinionated, in fact, that in the heat of the moment they would rather give up an otherwise good and profitable business than sway even an inch from their precious ideals. Disagreements *do* happen. And there are unfortunate times when they are so intense and of such magnitude that the continuation of the business is threatened. We don't live in a perfect world, after all.

Businesses, just like marriages, can end. Without planning the steps to take in the event of a monumental disagreement, your business could very well be headed for disaster.

Disaster

Rule #1: Disaster will inevitably strike.

Whether you have reason to fear a hurricane or a fifteen minute power outage, your business – to sensationalize the term – is headed for disaster. All of the proceeding D's, along with the one that follows, can be described as disasters. An angry ex-spouse, after all, is oftentimes more capable of tearing down the walls and uprooting the foundations of your business than any class 5 hurricane.

However, it is not our intention to classify these specific disasters. Hopefully, we've already adequately completed that task within the proceeding pages. For the purposes of this segment, it is our intent to define disaster as an act of nature.

Anyone living on the west coast – specifically, southern California – knows that earthquakes can happen on what seems like a daily basis. Each one represents the potential to both literally and figuratively break your business apart. All across the country, the elements stack up to toy with even the most steadfast of companies. Your family business runs the risk of being mutilated by winds, fires, floods, or any other encroaching elements.

Fortunately, not much needs to be said on how to mitigate the problem of disaster. Keep your business properly insured and you won't need to worry about it blowing away in the wind.

Depression

Those who have never suffered from depression may be wondering why this topic deserves to be included with the other D's. We didn't include depression just because the number six has a better ring to it than the number five. Depression is debilitating – every bit as debilitating as disability; every bit as serious as divorce or death; and every bit as damaging as disagreement or disaster.

The other awful truth connected to depression is that it is often the direct result of one of the other dangerous D's. Death and divorce are difficult enough for a business to overcome. Throw in a serious case of depression, and you've got one – or perhaps, more accurately, a series of giant hurdles to overcome.

We've already mentioned the worst part about depression: it's difficult to detect and often goes undiagnosed. What's more is that one simply cannot predict the outcome or end of a deep case of depression – if it can be expected to end at all.

Depression can directly affect a person's confidence and competence – which, when combining the two, often serves well to render a leader completely ineffective. It can destroy the morale of both the suffering individual and his/her coworkers, sometimes completely permeating the entire office. When a person feels depressed, he/she often loses the desire to complete everyday tasks. Work ethic and productivity can drop significantly.

Because it is so widely misunderstood, most business owners do not fear the effects of depression quite like they should. It *is* a real threat to good business. And you owe it to yourself to ensure that, just as you have in planning for all other dangers, all the necessary steps have been taken.

The Answers!

Now that we've highlighted the finer points of everything that a small business owner should fear, we can move on to the several ways to combat the dangerous D's.

Many of the aforementioned D's can be mitigated by proper planning. Both of the key ingredients to this planning have been alluded to already: adequate insurance and a well-documented buy/sell agreement. These two elements serve to aid in the often difficult process of splitting the rights to a business among two or more interested parties (should it ever come to that), passing interests to the next generation, and providing compensatory financing in the event of disaster. All of the first four D's – death, divorce, disability, and disagreement – may be covered by a buy/sell agreement.

And now perhaps we've talked too long about the buy/sell agreement without providing a proper definition. We oblige: Buy/sell agreements are capable of preserving the value and control of a particular business at the death, divorce, disability, or retirement of the owner. Furthermore, the agreement ensures that the owner – or the estate of the owner, should he/she die – will be paid adequately and accurately for his/her interest in the business and that either the surviving owners or his/her legally established successors will maintain ownership and control of the business. Reads like a lot of legal hoopla. You see now why we put off the task of defining it for so long.

The bad news about buy/sell agreements is that, like anything, they take proper funding to complete. The good news is that life insurance policies taken out on the owners can and will fund the agreements.

But before we get into that, we should establish that there are two different kinds of buy/sell agreements – and that it is important for you to understand the distinction. We will begin by covering the more difficult-to-explain of the two versions: the Entity Purchase Buy/Sell Agreement. We like to cast humility aside and think of ourselves as belonging to the more diligent stock, after all.

In order to more effectively highlight the workings of each agreement, we will use the event of death as our sample illustration. The relationship of the buy/sell agreement to the rest of the dangerous D's will be explained later in greater detail.

The Entity Purchase Buy/Sell Agreement

In order to give you the heads up for any additional research that you may decide to embark upon – or perhaps to just confuse things further – we should point out that the Entity Purchase Buy/Sell Agreement is also known as a Stock Redemption Agreement when dealing specifically with buy/sells on the corporate level. But, as we are assuming that you are dealing with a small family owned business, for the purposes of this segment, we will stick to the original title of Entity Purchase.

This type of buy/sell agreement is particularly useful when there are multiple owners involved – or, at least, multiple people who stand to benefit from the proceeds gathered from the sale of the business. The terms of this agreement stipulate that the owners, upon death, must agree to sell their respective interests in the business to the business itself. This requires the business – otherwise known as the "entity", hence the title of the agreement – to pay for and act as beneficiary of a life insurance policy on each acting owner.

Drawing upon our continuing anecdote, here's how an Entity Purchase Buy/Sell Agreement works: If the Brown family had managed to complete an Entity Purchase Agreement, upon

Tom's death, Brown Brothers Trucking would have received the life insurance proceeds. The business, in turn, would have been required to transfer those proceeds to the estate of Tom Brown – i.e. Darlene. Darlene's stock in the company would then be transferred back to the company itself. Harold could have then used this available stock to attract a new partner to help run things.

Financially speaking – at least on the pocketbooks of a company's individual owners – this is the more painless of the two types of agreements to make. It does, however, potentially hold two significant drawbacks: First, the surviving owners do not gain any control of the company upon the death of a stockholder – you'll notice, that the stock is paid for by and then transferred to the company itself; and, second, the insurance proceeds that help the company pay for the stock may be subject to heavier-than-desired taxation.

The Cross Purchase Buy/Sell Agreement

A Cross Purchase Buy/Sell Agreement begins with an understanding among the owners and successors of a particular business that, in the event of death, each owner is required to sell their individual interest in the company to either the surviving owners or one specific successor.

What makes this different from the Entity Purchase Buy/Sell Agreement is the way in which it is funded. In order to pay for this type of arrangement through life insurance, each *owner* – rather than the business itself – must purchase and be the beneficiary of a policy covering each of the other owners. Obviously, depending on how a business is divided and controlled, this could require a hefty sum of life insurance payments on the part of each owner – as he/she would need to own and pay for many several policies in order to ensure that he/she is compensated for the loss of a business partner.

The way that this agreement works is fairly similar to the Entity Purchase Agreement. Upon an owner's death, the insurance company pays benefits directly to the surviving owners. As per the typical agreement, the owners then pay the estate of the deceased partner in exchange for his/her interest in the business.

If they are willing to shoulder the initial financial burden, this can be a slightly more attractive buy/sell agreement in the eyes of the surviving owners. Because they are essentially purchasing the stock of their deceased partner at market value, they gain some ground – a greater portion of ownership – in the business. Any owners that, upon retirement, plan to sell their interest – to a successor within the family, let's say – will have actually reduced their taxable gain.

~~~

It may be difficult for you to assess which plan is best for you. For this reason, it is important that you consult a competent and experienced attorney. He/she can help you to draft a comprehensive plan that will ensure that your family business doesn't falter when faced with any legal and financial crossroads.

Now that we've defined what a buy/sell agreement is in relationship to death – and outlined the in's and out's of each type to consider – we can move on to explain how, coupled with the proper insurance products, the rest of the dangerous D's can be easily circumvented.

Divorce and the Buy/Sell Agreement

Before we begin to explain the relationship of divorce to the buy/sell agreement, it is important to note that, in the case of divorce, there is no divisible interest. Things can be paid for and departing parties can be compensated, but no business can be expected to continue after being split equally down the middle.

A buy/sell agreement can stipulate that a family business can compensate or eliminate an ex-spouse from control. It can also legally provide that, upon divorce, the ex-spouse is no longer entitled to his/her interest in the business. The method chosen varies depending upon the division of ownership, the circumstances of the marriage, and the interests of the company as a whole. Consult an attorney to discuss which method is right for you.

Most of the time, in the case where one spouse was the majority owner of the business before the marriage took place, it may be easier – legally speaking – and less financially draining to draft a plan indicating that divorce renders all business interests gained through the marriage completely void. Otherwise, the owner and any of his/her remaining partners could be forced to pay a large sum in order to buy out the interests of the departing spouse.

Disability and the Buy/Sell Agreement

Disability, like death, is a dangerous D that is most effectively avoided by employing a combination of a buy/sell agreement and a sufficient amount of insurance. Both are essential. In the event that a business owner or partner becomes disabled and incapable of completing his/her daily tasks, without a buy/sell agreement, the healthy owners or successors may be obligated to pay their disabled partner a salary while receiving nothing in return. The disabled partner, therefore, becomes little more than an economic drain on the company. If there is a buy/sell agreement in place, but no insurance, the remaining partners or successors would be forced to buy out their disabled partner with their own or their company's money – and the large sum of money that the typical buy-out requires may not be available.

The type of insurance necessary to avoid a danger such as this one is known as Disability Income Insurance. Sound familiar? This is because it is one type of insurance that every family business must consider at one point or another. Often, it is the last insurance policy that a company takes out. Perhaps, however – considering the fairly high risk of disability – it should be the first policy on your docket.

But why do we avoid such an obvious necessity? The answer is simple: no one wants to think of the potential for disability. In fact, if you asked 100 family business owners, age 50, whether or not they thought they would become disabled, 100 of them would most assuredly say "not me." Some of that 100 may be able to admit that they may, in fact, die someday – maybe – but none would admit to the potential for disability that we all share.

It's a startling fact to think about – all those family owned businesses completely unprepared for this dangerous D; especially when just as many businesses are utterly ruined by the effects of disability as are by the case of sudden and unforeseen death.

If we look back to the Brown brothers, again, we see that business-ending disaster could have been avoided had the brothers taken several key steps to cover their backs. We know already that the two did not have a working buy/sell agreement – so we will ignore that fault for the moment – but, had they decided to apply for a simple Disability Income Insurance policy, Harold would have been compensated and perhaps able to hire new help to carry on the family business. And in a business like theirs, one would think that Disability Income Insurance would have been made a top priority. After all, lifting heavy containers of milk several feet in the air into the back of a truck – without any help – carries a high risk of injury.

By now you should realize the importance of the buy/sell agreement. Let us now urge you to consider Disability Income Insurance. Disability could strike any of us at any time. Because of this potential, the time to take out a policy for your family business is now – or at least after you've finished reading this chapter/book – because if you wait until you're injured or diagnosed with a debilitating disease, it is too late.

Disagreement and the Buy/Sell Agreement

Yes we're aware of the absurdity of this segment title – 'disagreement' and 'agreement' within the same six word heading is a little odd. But it's important to talk about the relationship between the two. People can be proud. People can be stubborn. Disagreements have the tendency to escalate to the level of catastrophic, especially when you consider that you've chosen to mix family with business. The combination, unless properly planned for, can be deadly. Before a business-threatening disagreement rises up to challenge you – while things are still at least relatively civil between you, your business partners, and your successors – you must draft a detailed disagreement-related buy/sell agreement. One that everyone can agree on.

There are not many legally binding ways to handle a disagreement-related buy/sell agreement. Obviously, for a disagreement to be of any significance, it must threaten the success and continuation of the business in the most absolute sense. Everyone must come to the conclusion that, unless the two disagreeing parties are separated, the business will die. Before the disagreement occurs you may decide to compose a document, agreed upon and signed by all of your partners and successors, indicating the steps that will be taken in the event that disagreements simply cannot be resolved.

We will now move on to disaster. Most of the time, in the case of natural disaster, owners of family businesses do not seek to split the business up or buy out individual partners but, rather, they wish to repair the damages and carry on. Since this is the case, we will discuss disaster only as it relates to insurance.

Insuring Against Disaster

Most people understand the importance of property insurance. We all recognize that our businesses are not, in fact, flame retardant. Or waterproof. The first insurance policy that we all tend to sign, therefore, is one that will compensate for the physical loss of our business interests. And this is all well and good. Property insurance is very important. It does offset the economic – and, therefore, much of the stress – impact of this and many of the other dangerous D's.

But here's the kicker that most folks don't think about: in the event of a fire or other natural disaster, will you be able to maintain – financially speaking – while your business is rebuilt. Remember, the fire didn't just destroy your building; it destroyed its ability to function as a business and, as a result, your ability to collect a steady income. Property insurance may have kept your business from dying, but it can't prevent the effects of the six-month coma that it is likely to suffer.

Fortunately, there is an insurance product available that will help you to keep your head above water as they pump out the flooded foundations of your family business. This product is known as Business Interruption Insurance. It works just like Disability Income Insurance – in that it recognizes that you are unable to work for a salary, compensating for the loss of your paycheck.

Business Interruption Insurance carries one other unfortunate similarity to Disability Income Insurance: most business owners don't realize that it even exists or, if they do, pass it off as an unnecessary expense. Ask yourself the question, "Am I comfortable enough financially to go six months to a year without an income in the event of a natural disaster?" If the answer is "yes", then perhaps Business Interruption Insurance is an unnecessary expense. But, if you're like the majority of American family business owners, you depend on that salary to carry you from day to day.

Now, hopefully, we have reached an understanding. You never know what can happen so be sure to take all the necessary precautions to protect yourself from the worst. Now that we've covered the heavy stuff, let's take a deep cleansing breath and shift our focus. We now invite you to join us as we explain the many components that you must consider in order to ensure that your business transitions smoothly from one generation to the next. Read on and learn how to craft your own unique blueprint for the future.

Chapter 3

Estate Planning Issues

You might be asking yourself, why should I be reading about this most unpleasant of subjects? It's funny; everyone seems to love to discuss death – just so long as it's not their own death. Facing mortality is one of those issues always confined to the backburner. For some, it can be quite painful to ponder, let alone discuss.

Unfortunately, estate planning may actually be an intensely critical element to your succession plan. And, as such, we were forced to drop this chapter into the book.

But before we dive headlong into the luxuriously large swimming pool that is estate planning, we must first point out that the topics covered within this chapter are broad enough to account for a book in themselves. We merely plan to touch on each subject. You'll have to wait with bated breath for our follow-up book on Estate Planning Issues. We're sure it will be a page-turner.

On this same note, it is important for you to realize that no two estates are the same. Even if we were the nation's leading authorities on estate planning – and you can rest assured that we are not – it would be impossible for us to outline the correct plan for you, the individual and unique reader, within these pages. The contents of this chapter, instead, should be regarded as a kind of primer. Though it won't reveal all the answers, it will give you an arsenal of questions to lob at your advisors. And when we say advisors, we mean your (of course, highly competent) attorney, accountant, and financial advisor. Certified Financial Planners (CFPs) are also highly qualified to help you sift through the complex legal vernacular that is estate planning and tax law and offer advice on the most relevant strategies for both you and your family business.

Why Is This Important?

Ah; good question. Failing to plan your estate means that, upon your death, your family – specifically your intended heirs – will be left with little or no direction or control over what happens to the estate you've left behind.

There are several actions that your state government can and will take in the event that you left no specific instructions regarding the distribution of your estate to your heirs. The actions are as follows:

- The state will enforce its intestacy laws.

Each state has laws designed to distribute your estate in the absence of a valid will. These intestacy laws are different in each state, so be sure to consult a good lawyer or accountant. If your procrastination keeps you from seeking legal advice and drafting a will, your state has a plan for you and your family. Essentially, these laws allow the state government to "draft a will for you". It's entirely possible that your survivors will be less than pleased with the version that are presented with, too.

If you have a surviving spouse and/or children, state law will dictate which survivors receive their proportionate share. For example, your spouse may receive anywhere from 25% to 75% of your estate, depending on your state of residence. The children, then, inherit the rest. This may seem logical, but consider for a moment the prospect of a young child (for example) owning property or heading a company. Scary, huh? The courts, most likely, will have this same view. And, as such, they will probably take steps to impede the management of your former company in an effort to protect the rights of your son or daughter.

- The court will appoint an executor or administrator for your estate.

This is a problem because there is no way of knowing who this person will be. The benefit of naming an executor within your will is that you have the power to name someone whom you know and trust. A court-appointed executor will know nothing about your family and their needs – except what can be revealed in numbers and figures on the pages provided by the probate court. How can you be certain that this person will do what is best for your heirs?

Furthermore, since this person was court appointed, he/she may be forced to take out an expensive bond in order to insure your estate. He/she is legally bound to do so. If you had appointed your own executor, this would not have been necessary and the money used to cover the insuring bond could have been passed on to your heirs.

- If both you and your spouse die while your children are still young, the court will appoint a guardian to care for them.

Imagine a total stranger raising your children. It is a chilling thought. Without a proper estate plan, in the event of the premature death of you and your spouse, your children could be raised by someone other than the close friend, trusted family member, or godparent of your choice.

- If your children are under 18 when you die, there are a great number of problems created by the state.

Among these problems is the fact that since your child is legally under age the court maintains jurisdiction over the estate and all of its assets. Your child's representative may be forced to account for the estate value at least once every year – costing a great deal of inheritance money in accounting and court fees. Furthermore, as soon as the child turns 18, the court hands over full control of the estate. What's so wrong with this? How many 18-year-olds possess the knowledge and responsibility needed to handle and maintain a large inheritance? Without a proper guardian or outside advice, your child may burn through the inheritance and wind up in worse position than he/she would have been if the money had never come his/her way.

- The court will divide your estate among your heirs as it sees fit – regulations vary from state to state.

As mentioned, for the most part, states loosely follow a model of distribution for inheritance. In the event that you are survived by both a spouse and children, in many states, half the estate goes to the spouse and half is divided equally among the children. In the event that your spouse is deceased as well, the entire estate goes to your children. The opposite is true if you are survived only by a spouse. In the event that there is no surviving spouse or children, the estate is divided between parents and/or siblings and other descendents.

If you haven't guessed already, our advice would be to plan thoroughly and accurately – unless of course you do not mind having the government do the work for you later on down the road.

The Process

There is a process to estate planning that is complicated enough to warrant its own specific segment. Though the issues associated with each estate vary from person to person, the succession of steps-to-take can and should be etched in stone. Be sure to both ponder upon and discuss these steps with your bevy of competent advisors. We have authored a process that will show you *where* to step – your advisors, then, can show you *how*.

Gather Data

This common first step isn't just reserved for scientists; it works in the world of finance too. This may be time consuming but, without it, you will not be able to make effective decisions and outline the proper goals for your individual estate. Furthermore, if you plan to discuss the outlook and potential for your estate with your team of advisors, you must have all of the ingredients at hand before you can even begin. Prescription without proper diagnosis is malpractice.

It is also important that, however tedious the process of gathering information may be, you take efforts to include every iota of pertinent data. Missing bits and pieces may lead to significant mistakes down the road.

The basic information you may need to gather includes: the last three years of state and federal tax returns; the last three years profit and loss statements and net worth statements; all insurance policies; all bank statements; all statements of your investments; all statements from all retirement plans and IRAs. Dig through the file cabinet at the office and at home. Go through the piles of "important papers to be filed" that you have stacked in boxes in the garage, in the basement, in the attic, in your climate controlled storage unit. You have the paperwork. Finding it can sometimes be the real chore. Your financial advisors can tell you if there is any piece of paper you're missing.

Establish Goals and Set Priorities

Just as with anything else in life – at least anything that has value – you must clearly establish your goals and priorities;

both for yourself and to your advisors. Nothing progresses without a definitive track to follow. Your family business, for example, would never have reached its current state of stability and success if you hadn't established a viable set of goals in advance.

Unfortunately, since we're talking about finances and assets that surround a family, establishing goals and setting priorities is also a rather troublesome task. This is because whenever there are multiple parties involved or interested in one particular estate, disagreements are bound to arise. Consider the logistics of expecting your heirs, their spouses, and other beneficiary family members to agree on anything, let alone an estate in which they stand to benefit from. Again, this is why you should seek the council of an attorney, CPA, and financial advisor. The further you take the decision out of your own hands, the better off you and your family will be. At the very least, decisions can be made without you having to take all of the heat.

Some priorities you may want to consider include:

- Successfully avoiding as much taxation of your estate as possible

- Maximizing the total value of your assets that you plan to pass to your heirs

- Minimizing the costs of transferring your assets to your heirs

- Ensuring that your assets are properly distributed to their intended recipients after you are gone

- Taking steps to provide a sufficient amount of estate liquidity in order to pay estate settlement costs

After your feelings regarding all of these topics have been established, your advisors can recommend a series of actions to take. Be sure to secure ample time to highlight how your preferences relate to an effective plan before moving on to our third step.

Implement the Plan

Obviously, once the plan has been discussed and outlined, the next step is to put it into practice. As we have already drilled into your head, it is crucial that you correspond openly with your team of advisors both before, during, and – as we will get to later – after the estate plan has been put into action. In order to ensure that you are not making a minor mistake that will eventually lead to major problems for your heirs, competent legal, tax, and financial advice are absolutely mandatory. Yes, we said mandatory.

Transversely, most owners of a family business have a lot of other advice that will be hurled in their direction – advice that is best ignored. If the fact that you are in the process of drafting and implementing an estate plan is well known throughout your family – and, as we will discuss, we think it is essential that your family remains as informed as possible – you can practically count on receiving a whole slew of unsolicited and inadequate advice from well-meaning but (let's face it) amateur family members. This advice should be completely disregarded. Though your cousin Teddy may seem to have an excellent point about the potential horrors of probate court, the fact remains that he just doesn't have a notarized degree from an ABA accredited law school hanging on his wall. Odds are that Teddy is placing all of his trust in stories that he's heard and really doesn't have the slightest idea what he's talking about.

Monitor the Plan

This is perhaps the most important, and all-too-often overlooked, action to take regarding estate planning. Just because the building of a project has been completed does not mean that its needs have been handled for good. You didn't launch your business, for example, just to turn around and let it run itself. As you know, it would have run itself right into the ground. The same is true for your estate plan. It requires maintenance, observation, and adaptation. There are many influences that will require you to reevaluate and perhaps alter the foundations of your estate plan. These influences include – but are not exclusive to:

- Marriage

- Divorce

- Birth or adoption of children

- Significant changes in personal finances

- Tax law changes

Marriage and divorce are fairly obvious influences. Sometimes you don't know when either of them can occur. The addition or subtraction of a spouse from the equation has a significant influence on your estate plan and you will need to take action to redraft whenever either of these life events transpires. The same is true for the birth or adoption of a child. Obviously, adoption takes a great deal of pre-planning, so you're likely to see it coming long before the estate planning aspect becomes a problem, but unexpected births are quite different. Sometimes the arrival of a new child is a surprise – and, for many people, occurs later in life than desired. Whenever a new child comes into your family, you have a new heir to consider, and your estate plan should be altered accordingly.

Another aspect of life that is beyond the control of most people is significant change in personal finances. There are many influences on your financial wellbeing. Markets shift, business picks up or dries up, investors change their minds, exchange rates dip and peak – the business world, as you know, is highly unstable. Whenever there is a significant change thrust upon your business or your personal finances, your estate plan needs to be readdressed.

And, finally, we have listed tax law changes. We've saved this one for last because it is perhaps the most unpredictable influence on your estate plan. It is the very reason why you must be sure to reaffirm or rewrite your estate plan on a regular basis. To sum it up, the government is always changing its outlook on the issue of tax law. New leaders and double-speaking incumbents have a way of revising tax laws in order to suit the needs of their own particular candidacies. Be sure to discuss the changes and the *potential* changes with a competent attorney and/or CPA at least once a year or you may find that you end up with an ineffective and behind-the-times estate plan that will do your heirs more harm than good.

Concerning Wills

Though it is a reasonably well known term, we'll begin with the assumption that we need to reveal the meaning of the concept in question. A will is a valid legal document that addresses the disposition of one's property. It is perhaps the most simplistic way to ensure that one's property is passed on to specifically selected individuals, which we will refer to henceforth as "beneficiaries." Most states require that a will is recorded in writing, for obvious reasons. If there is a physical copy of your will (signed by you) that can be taken into court, your dying intentions are far less likely to be met with valid opposition.

Essentially, a will is a court-approved vehicle for you to pass your assets on to the beneficiary or beneficiaries of choice. Completing and ensuring that your will is properly implemented is a difficult task, however. Also, legal precedents that surround this particular type of document tend to make the issue a little more dubious than we've let on so far. Wills have their ups and downs; their positives and negatives. Let's address what a will can do, then move on to what it cannot do, what kind of maintenance is required, its relationship to probate, and, finally, what happens if you decide to avoid drafting a will altogether.

What a Will Can Do

If you do, in fact, care about where and with whom your assets end up after your death, a will is a remarkably useful tool. The following is a list of things that a will can do:

- Relate specific bequests to a spouse, children, or other designated beneficiaries

- Distribute cash or property to a non-profit organization

- Transfer property to predetermined trusts

- Establish an executor; who will help determine proper distribution of assets according to the provisions of the will

For those who are fairly familiar with the concept of wills, these points may seem like no-brainers. We've all seen mock readings of wills as they have been portrayed on television or in movies – the irresponsible and unlikely son/daughter receives the bulk of the family fortune while the assuming older sibling is basically snubbed, leading to great intrigue and/or comedy. While there is a fair deal of truth behind the legal process that is revealed onscreen, things are not necessarily as cut and dried as they seem.

It should be pointed out that wills are commonly misunderstood. They are not, in fact, the legal lockboxes that they are made out to be. Wills are valuable because the above four points are crucial to any estate plan – however, it is important to realize that these categories are all that wills do. They serve no other purpose. In fact, there is a great deal more with which a will is commonly and erroneously associated.

What a Will Cannot Do

Many people draft wills and leave it at that, possibly dooming their estates to complex and costly litigation. In hopes of clearing things up, we provide the following list of things that a will cannot do:

- A will cannot specifically exclude a spouse (in most states).

So we begin with the juicy subject of excluding a spouse. That's right, even if you really didn't care much for him/her during your lifetime, your spouse is legally entitled to a portion of your assets upon your death. The size of the portion varies from state to state, but the underlying message is the same: No matter how hard you try, your will cannot be drawn to slight your spouse. This is due largely to the fact that, however passive his/her role might have been, marriage is a legally binding contract and the credit for whatever you have earned in life is divided between the bound parties.

- A will cannot provide excessive gifts to charities if the decedent is survived by a spouse or children.

You might be an extraordinarily charitable man/woman but, under the strength of a will alone (pun intended), you cannot expect to leave the majority of your estate to a non-profit organization if you are survived by a spouse or children. As above, state law stipulates that your spouse or immediate descendents are entitled to a significant portion of your estate. There are several more flexible estate planning options for you to consider if you do desire to leave the majority of your assets to charity – fear not, more on charitable giving will be discussed in later chapters.

- A will cannot disinherit a child without a specific intention to do so.

A mouth full, we know – and perhaps overly so. Allow us to rephrase: You can't accidentally leave a child out of the will. If you really don't want your estranged son/daughter to receive even a small slice of your estate, you must clearly and specifically give directions to exclude him/her. This prevents any unintentional oversights from occurring – because, due to the relative finality of wills, simply forgetting to include a child can be rather disastrous.

- A will is not an iron-clad, final-word document that will be held up in court.

We realize that this bullet point kind of contradicts the final sentence of the previous paragraph. There is no such thing as the absolute finality of a will (hence the use of the word "relative"). Contesting a will does take a great deal of effort, however. The important point here is that it is not an infallible document. Its stipulations can, in fact, be fought and overturned in court.

- A will should not divulge the decedent's desired funeral plans.

So why do so many people insist on including them? Applying simple logic should be enough to prevent a person from wasting time on including his/her funeral agenda within the final will. Wills are almost always read *after* the funeral is long over. Not much use for your burial requests once you have already been buried.

- A will does not allow your estate and your heirs to avoid the probate process.

This is perhaps the biggest inadequacy of wills – and probably one of the main reasons why many adequately-informed business owners avoid focusing their estate plans on this particular document. Those two little words (Probate Court) are just about enough to give even the most confident business owner a strong case of the howling fantods. What most do not realize, however, is that the probate process actually has some positives. More on this topic later on in the chapter.

Will-Maintenance

We have already covered the significance of performing regular check-ups on your estate plan, but let it be known that these specific reasons to perform the check-ups also apply to the will. In addition to the outside influences such as marriage or divorce, birth or adoption of children, tax law changes, and significant changes in personal finances, there is at least one important relationship-related factor with which to contend. Simply put: your relationships constantly change in capacity and intensity.

Hypothetically speaking, you may wind up making amends with that estranged son/daughter or you might one day gain a son-in-law who is more like a son than an in-law. People have a tendency to become either more or less deserving of a large portion of your estate over the course of a lifetime. For this and the previously mentioned reasons, it is critical that you revisit your will at least once a year. Otherwise, your assets might end up in the wrong places.

Caring for a will is a fairly simple process. All it takes is a regular meeting with a qualified and trusted attorney. The attorney may have a specific agenda to cover, points to address or amend, and other actions to take.

What If You Don't Draft a Will?

Oh, fire and pestilence. Do draft a will. Even if you see it as a fairly feeble attempt to pass your estate, tax free, to your heirs – which, we must admit, is an astute observation – it still carries weight within an effective estate plan. This is because, as previously mentioned, without proper directives, the court in your state will be forced to provide a will for you. This agenda is known as the "laws of descent." Without proper planning, the laws of descent will determine the distribution of your cash and property.

And what are the odds of your particular preferences matching exactly to the cold divisible logic of the state? Probably zero. Regardless of how you feel about wills – and regardless of your financial situation – it is extremely advisable that you draft a will.

~~~

The bottom line is that wills have different effects on different estates. There are a wide range of opinions within the legal community regarding whether or not wills are advantageous. As we have mentioned again and again, it is important that you discuss the relevance of wills with your attorney. More than any book, he/she is well within position to provide sound advice on the subject.

Concerning Trusts

Many advisors will suggest that a trust is the most effective way to plan your estate if you feel that probate court and the fees that it entails are entirely negative. We don't blame you if you do feel this way – desiring to save money and preserve wealth for your heirs is a valid motivation.

And what is a trust? Trusts take many forms but, by and large, the term refers to a legal document that relates specific instructions regarding the ownership and management of all the property titled in the name of the trust itself. The common trust requires three separate parties to uphold its value.

The first party is you – or you and your spouse. Though it sounds like a term ripped from the pages of a poorly written science fiction novel, you are known as the "trustmaker." Simply enough, this is because you make the trust. Some people also like to refer to the trustmaker as the "trustor" – but since we much prefer the gravity and/or comic appeal of the former title, we'll just stick to that one.

The second party is known as the "trustee" – with the inflection on the last syllable, thereby separating it from the antiquated and slightly underappreciated adjective "trusty." The trustee, though the name does not imply it, is often a collective group of people – if not a formally elected person, it is often an institution or a bank that is appointed by the trustmaker and charged with the task of carrying out the instructions of the trust. Think of the trustee as the keeper of the trust.

The third and final party is known as the beneficiary. We have already introduced you to this term, so we won't dwell on it long. As mentioned before, the beneficiary is the person who benefits from inheriting the trust – hence the name. When setting up the trust, the trustmaker or grantor chooses his/her beneficiaries.

Trusts have been around for hundreds of years. During that time, lawyers have managed to divide them into several different types and factions. Each type has its own variation on the above model – and we will address the properties unique to a select few of the types, accordingly. Be warned, there are many different types of trusts; you may need to do additional research. We have only included the broadest terms.

Revocable Trusts

A revocable trust is also sometimes called a "revocable living trust." We'll employ the shorter term in order to save typing time on our part and reading time on yours. Whatever name it goes by, it is the kind of trust that is subject to change according to the demands of the trustmaker. Updates, revisions, and even cancellations may take place at any time. Due to its remarkable flexibility, this is a fairly popular kind of trust.

As with anything else in this book, and in life, revocable trusts have their ups and downs. Since we are positive thinkers, we'll start with the truly attractive aspects of this type of trust:

- The trustmaker and the trustee can be the same person.

That's right, there's no need for a bank when you're dealing with revocable trusts. In fact, this is regarded as a legal, but highly personal document. Unlike most other estate planning tactics, revocable trusts are not a public decree. You're your own trustee.

- The trustee (i.e. you and/or your spouse) maintains full legal control over all property listed in the name of the trust.

The reason that this is such a sweet deal is because you, the trustee, can own and operate any and every asset held within the trust while, at the same time, not having to fear the process of probate court (for your heirs) after your death. A revocable trust, in a sense, is just an extension of yourself. While living, everything titled in its name is controlled by you and, after your death, is not subject to probate.

- The trustee can include valuable instructions regarding the trust.

Many things can be determined by a trust. Some valuable instructions include who the beneficiary or beneficiaries will be upon the trustmaker/trustee's death, who will be the trustee's successor, and what happens to the trust in the event that the trustee becomes disabled or is determined mentally unfit to handle the decision making associated with trust management.

- Trusts can cross state lines.

This means that all valuables held within a trust, regardless of where they are in the US – they could be scattered across seven states, for example – are still only subject to one (if any) probate proceeding. This is obviously an attractive feature for people with large tracts of land or complex family businesses that fall in several different states. It is a way to synergize even the most complex of inheritances and ensure that all beneficiaries benefit as much as possible.

- Because they are so private, they're tough to attack.

Revocable trusts are not public documents. Aunt Martha, who might have every reason to be disgruntled about your estate plan, will have a much tougher time backing up her claims in court. Unlike wills, revocable trusts are not publicly filed or easily accessed.

We now shift to the negatives of a revocable trust. Though few in number, these negatives are certainly not short on significance. They are as follows:

- Revocable trusts cannot be used to avoid income or estate tax.

Why so many people believe the contrary is beyond us. Assets held within a Revocable Trust are every bit as subject to income and estate tax as anything else in your possession.

- Revocable trusts will not protect your assets from creditors either before or after your death.

Again, this is a common misconception associated with revocable trusts. To sum it up, since you maintain full control of the trust, creditors have every right to pursue it. You still legally own the assets within, therefore, they are subject to the claims of creditors.

So, essentially, revocable trusts are an excellent way to pass your assets on to your beneficiaries while avoiding probate and the legal fees associated with probate but they just do not offer the asset protection that some would have you believe. If protection and avoidance of taxation is your goal, the following solution provides more support.

Irrevocable Trusts

Irrevocable trusts, as the name implies, are trusts that cannot be changed once the creation is done. During the lifetime of the trustmaker, the trust cannot be altered or cancelled. So, essentially, we simply flip-flop several of the positives with the negatives of revocable trusts.

The benefits that irrevocable trusts share with revocable trusts include avoidance of probate, right to privacy, and ability to include assets held within several different states. In addition to these positives, we can also include:

- Potential avoidance of estate taxes.

Placing property into an irrevocable trust is considered a completed gift – and, usually, this is enough to remove the property from the taxable estate. This doesn't make it entirely tax-free, however. All assets placed into the trust may still be subject to gift tax liability according to the value of the "gift."

- Protection from creditors.

As previously mentioned, assets placed into an irrevocable trust are considered completed gifts. Since these "gifts," in essence, no longer belong to you, they may be free from attack and litigation carried out by your creditors.

If you haven't already guessed, the main problem with an irrevocable trust is that it doesn't offer the kind of freedom and overall flexibility that is offered by a revocable trust. Once it's put into place, there's no turning back.

Living v. Testamentary Trust

Trusts are often designated as either Living or Testamentary. As the names suggest, a living trust is established during the lifetime of the trustmaker and a testamentary trust is established upon his/her death. Both trusts that we have mentioned above are actually living trusts – therefore living trusts generally carry many of the aforementioned strengths and weaknesses of either a revocable or irrevocable trust. Living trusts are easy to start-up and require little on-going maintenance. They afford an extra measure of protection against loss of control, and ensure that your assets remain out of the public record even after your death. However, they do not provide protection against creditors or divorce, and do not reduce estate taxes for estates over $2 million in value ($4 million if married).

Testamentary trusts, however, are subject to a few more stipulations and restrictions which vary from state to state. Only a funded living trust avoids probate court. In a testamentary trust, property must pass into the trust by way of the will and, thus, must go through the probate court process. As always, our expert advice to you: Consult your attorney.

Concerning Titling and Ownership

Before any of the above actions can be taken – drafting wills, setting up trusts, etc. – ownership must be established by titling *all* assets. When things go before a judge, it is far better to have things legally and formally titled. Title everything. Go crazy with the titling. Or, more appropriately, title as much as and how your attorney advises.

But how? There are so many different ways to manage titles and provide for ownership. Too many, perhaps. The problem with so many choices is that even small mistakes in your titling and ownership plan can lead to huge problems for your beneficiaries. Another aspect that makes titling and ownership a particularly dicey subject is that it is critical for your selected methods of ownership to be compatible with your will or trust(s). It is so easy to make a mistake in your plan by having property owned in a way that does not contribute to your ultimate goal. For this reason, you must a) consult an attorney, accountant, and/or financial advisor and b) frequently review the ownership of land, homes, businesses, automobiles and other property.

Though there are many ways to hold title, it may be true that only one is right for your particular estate. The rest may do more harm than good. And keep in mind that every state is different. With cautionary reluctance, we provide the list anyway:

- Individual Ownership (or Fee Simple)

We've started with this one because it is the easiest to define. We're procrastinators at heart. Individual ownership is just like it sounds: there is only one owner – you. You maintain total legal control and rights to the asset. This may sound like a pretty decent deal but, believe us, in the event of credit problems or harmful litigation, "Fee Simple" can come back to haunt you.

- Joint Tenancy with Right of Survivorship

This is a rather cold and calculated way of saying "you all enjoy full control over the property." This is a method of ownership that is commonly used when there are more than two parties interested in the ownership of an asset. This is a popular route to take for family owned businesses, for example, when there are three or more senior partners within the family who have equal claim to the rights of the business itself. Essentially, all tenants attached to the title have full control over the asset. Each can feel free to buy or sell all or portions of the asset as though he/she were sole owner. When all but one of the tenants die, the surviving tenant is granted full rights to the asset in "Fee Simple."

- Tenancy In Common

This method of ownership is fairly similar to the above, only it divides rights and control over the asset into fractions. Each tenant claimed on the title has a share of the asset. The shares can be divided equally or staggered according to the tenants' needs. The tenants may decide that seniority calls for a large slice of the asset; or perhaps greater involvement in the maintenance and direction of the asset is what it takes to gain more controlling interest. It's entirely up to the title holders.

- Tenancy by the Entirety

This is a tactic that is commonly employed by married couples. Since the law suggests that the act of marriage is a legally binding decree – two become one – married couples can actually title their assets (specifically a home) as two people functioning as one. This means that, upon the death of the first spouse, the home or other asset is passed to the other, free of probate. This is because, even though a spouse is dead, the legally supported two-in-one entity is still represented by the surviving spouse.

- Life Estate

One of the most frequently used (and abused) estate planning techniques is the life estate. A life estate is very simple and cheap to create. All that is necessary to create a life estate is for the owner(s) of an asset to transfer title to the asset to another person, but retain the right to use, possess and control the asset during his or her lifetime. Life estates are most commonly used with real estate and are created by the owner of the real estate by signing and delivering a deed to the property to the person(s) that the owner wants to give it to, with a specific clause regarding life estate. They are beneficial in avoiding probate and medical assistance (nursing home) planning.

However, there are several significant adverse affects of a life estate if you have transferred your property to your children. There is, as you know, no such thing as a free lunch. Your attorney can provide you all the various scenarios of what could happen, but by creating a life estate, you are giving up control of your property and the only persons that will benefit from the transfer is the person you transfer the property to- not you. Some still decide it is advantageous, but seek proper counsel before you make your decision.

- Corporation (or other business entity)

Some assets may be titled under the name of the business which may or may not be beneficial for your heirs. It can make business sense to have vehicles titled under the company name as they are insured under the company name and are company assets. Most corporate assets should perhaps remain corporate assets even after the transition of power. It's important to make certain that your assets are titled correctly so they pass to your beneficiaries and heirs as you intend. You should review all of your beneficiary designations so they are up-to-date and consistent with your current plans. This helps assure that your wishes will be carried out because, while your will may state your intentions, the ownership and subsequent transfer of your assets may be legally dictated by how they are titled. What's the end-all, be-all word to the wise? See your attorney and get your assets titled correctly now.

The Terrible Taxes

Estate tax laws are always changing so we hesitate to include the following table. Please understand that this chart is intended to give you a simple inkling of how much Uncle Sam takes from your estate. We hope to wake you up – maybe even get a "Wow!" in there – to realize that planning your succession and your estate are the smartest business moves you ever made. Remember to consult your estate tax professional to get the latest information on taxes and credits.

Taxable Gift or Estate		Tentative Tax	
FROM	TO	Tax on Col. 1	Tax Rate on Excess
$0	$11,000	$0	18%
11,000	20,000	1,800	20%
20,000	40,000	3,800	22%
40,000	60,000	8,200	24%
60,000	80,000	13,000	26%
80,000	100,000	18,200	28%
100,000	150,000	23,800	30%
150,000	250,000	38,800	32%
250,000	500,000	70,800	34%
500,000	750,000	155,800	37%
750,000	1,000,000	248,300	39%
1,000,000	1,250,000	345,800	41%
1,250,000	1,500,000	448,300	43%
1,500,000	2,000,000	555,800	45%
2,000,000	+	780,800	46%

Key Credits and Deductions

Unified Credit

Again, this is the current information on estate tax credit and gift tax credit; it could be obsolete before the ink dries on the page. Be aware of the unified credit and ask your tax attorney about the best ways to reduce the burden of estate taxes.

Year	Max. Estate Tax Credit	Max. Gift Tax Credit	Max. Unified Rate
2002	$1 million	$1 million	50%
2003	$1 million	$1 million	49%
2004	$1.5 million	$1 million	48%
2005	$1.5 million	$1 million	47%
2006	$2 million	$1 million	46%
2007	$2 million	$1 million	45%
2008	$2 million	$1 million	45%
2009	$3.5 million	$1 million	45%
2010	Tax Repeal	Tax Repeal	0%
2011	$1 million	$1 million	50%
2012	$1 million	$1 million	50%
2013	$1 million	$1 million	50%

Marital Deduction

Some may hope to avoid estate taxes by leaving everything to the spouse, however all assets are taxed when your spouse dies at a higher bracket. Spouses can make unlimited gifts to his/her spouse during lifetime without incurring any gift tax. You can gift each child $12,000 per year and pay no gift tax. It may be something to consider, but again, check with your tax professional as the IRS changes the rules all the time.

Charitable Deduction

Another way to reduce estate taxes and do something worthwhile with your money is to leave some to charity. Money or property left to a qualifying charity is deductible from the gross estate. That is what we call a win-win situation: less to Uncle Sam and more to the betterment of the world. You decide what charitable organization(s) you believe in and you decide what amount goes to each. Your wishes are all in your will, and your team of advisors and your family are aware of your desires too of course. Or they will be as soon as you finish reading this book.

More on charitable giving will be covered in later chapters. As we have mentioned, this primer on estate planning is in no way comprehensive. In fact, these pages haven't even begun to scratch the surface. There are many other ways to shape your estate according to your desires – and, before you put any of the above plans into action, you must seek the sage advice of your team of advisors.

~~~

While you can never completely eliminate estate taxes, you can effectively reduce them with different types of trusts. Planning is a must. Let us repeat: Planning is a must. Without proper planning, the tax bill could be almost impossible to pay. Businesses, remember, are very rarely just simple assets that can be liquidated. Even if portions of the firm can be sold, the simple act of selling will invariably hurt – if not destroy – the company's productivity. Furthermore, the government only allows nine months time to pay off what is owed. Don't allow your legacy to become an estate tax nightmare for your family. Talk to your team of advisors and evaluate your estate tax plan periodically to keep up with the changes.

Chapter 4

Family Communications

− You must run a family business like a business, not a family.

Transferring a business to another person can be emotionally, financially, and often mentally and physically draining. Throw in the fact that you intend to pass your business on to a family member and we have several major dilemmas to unfurl. If you've managed to leaf through the book to this point, the thought has probably already occurred to you that passing your business to the next generation without any glitches will be an extremely difficult if not impossible task.

Let us be the first to tell you that your worries are absolutely founded. You *do* have a lot to be concerned about. Statistics suggest that fewer than one in three businesses are successfully passed from their founders to the founder's children. And even the handful of businesses that do make it across one generational gap almost always fail to cross another. It's the age-old shirt sleeves to shirt sleeves proverb: The first generation moves out of the factory and champions a growing family business; the second generation takes that business and expands the wealth to the point where it plateaus; the third generation inherits the wealth, burning it admirably; and the fourth generation, dirt poor, is forced to head back to the factory.

This may seem like a rather broad estimate of the typical family business. How could we possibly make such bold statements? Because there are many negative factors that have survived the test of time, corrupting business after business, dooming them to failure.

And what about the dangerous D's? We've already dedicated an entire chapter to their illumination so we won't spend too much time dwelling on the subject here. They always come up at the wrong times – maybe while your business is in the process of passing from your hands to the successor's. Just remember that they're out there. Lurking.

There are ways to beat the historical trend of failure and become one of those select few families who maintain affluence throughout centuries, let alone generations. There are reasons why the Rockefellers, Carnegies, and Hearsts of the world are still household names.

Remember, building your business to the point of success wasn't easy. Harmonizing your family and preparing your business to be passed won't be easy either. Read on, but be forewarned: Getting a family to agree on anything can be a chore; getting a family to wrap its collective head around your intentions for the business can be downright overwhelming. So we offer you (with a drum roll please):

The #1 Most Overwhelming Question Every Family Business Owner Must Face When Passing the Business to the Next Generation

How can I pass the business to one family member or another and ensure that the rest of the family doesn't resent me for it? How do I maintain relative harmony among the most interested parties?

It is so overwhelming it is actually two questions. The simple answer to both questions is that there is absolutely no way to maintain relative harmony or avoid resentment when it comes to extended family. We're talking about people who still hold grudges based solely upon the fact that they weren't chosen to host the annual reunion in 1987. Why should your decision about the succession of your business be any different? If you haven't planned well in advance – and made that plan known to everyone in the family – expect some dissention in the ranks. Fortunately, there is a salve for every wound.

Building Harmony, Respect, and Understanding

So how do you pass the business on to a loved one and avoid being resented by the rest of the family? There is no simple answer to this question, to be sure. Mild jealousy is common to even the most tight-knit of extended families. Also, add to this the fact that any time a singular leader makes a major decision, no matter what the setting, second-guessing from the followers is all but a certainty.

In fact, it is exactly this concept that leads us to our first solution to the problem. The only way to avoid being resented by the non-inheriting members of your extended family is to take yourself out of the role of the lone, infallible leader. In other words, the more people you allow to maintain at least some responsibility for the company – however small – the less likely you are to have the proverbial finger pointed in your direction.

This isn't to say that you should feel obligated to delegate direct control to other key members of your family. Just take steps to make them feel more involved. Create a mock board of family members that have the power to consult with you on matters such as charitable donations or building a family mission statement.

Family Mission Statement

Family mission statement? That's right. Mission statements aren't just for businesses anymore. Successful family units – especially those centered by a successful family business – often adhere to the same kind of mission statements at home as at work. Why is this? Introducing formal elements like a mission statement into a family seems like a rather cold and calculated measure. Actually, it's just the opposite – it's perhaps the most caring and worthwhile action that any family can take.

The central quality to any successful business or family is unity and understanding. Everyone needs to work together to achieve a common goal. Common goals tend to give groups a sense of purpose, a *meaning* – and a family business isn't worth anything if there is no meaning behind it. Without a common bond to spur it along, the only thing it is good for is creating disruption.

The family mission statement builds harmony among family members because it embodies the summation of each contributing person's financial, intellectual, and personal goals and, as it is passed down over the years, builds respect and understanding among future generations. Family mission statements have a way of encouraging cohesion. If everyone has a say in its creation, it will be a body of text that commands the respect for the family and the family business from each of the contributing members.

The family mission statement is so powerful because it is both the expression of an interconnected identity and a means of reflecting unified goals that allow the family to prosper and learn. It is the embodiment of ancestors' accomplishments and aspirations and a beacon to success for future generations. It is value – worth, by very nature. And you must remember that even more valuable than your business and wealth, even more important than leadership skills or confidence or pride, is the sense of one's self-worth. It is indeed the only truly priceless gift that you can pass to the next generation.

Drafting the Mission

Crafting a mission statement, however, is no easy task. What's more, the process of gathering information is different from family to family. Families with just two parents and young children will require a much more simplified approach than a broad multigenerational clan. For the former, all it really takes is teamwork and understanding between two individuals – individuals that allow the children to take part in amending and adapting the family mission statement as they grow into adults – but, for the latter, the process is much more complicated.

The first and most important point about crafting a family mission statement is that things should never be etched in stone. Values, needs, and goals constantly change – and the mission statement needs to remain in flux, becoming more complex or narrow as the times demand. Both time and numbers have the tendency to affect even the most encompassing of mission statements. Time brings new occurrences and influences that can shake the foundations of our values. New generations are born. Older generations die. Thus, the best family mission statements are adaptable – they evolve with the family.

Even though the surface and volume of every mission statement is ever-changing, the roots should always remain the same. The roots are strong and unwavering – and should contain the following key points:

1. The rules governing the interaction of family members

2. An outline of the values shared by the family

3. A decree of the responsibility of each family member to maintain open lines of communication

4. A summary of the three essential categories of family goals

The compilation of all this information can either be generalized to make a traditional mission statement or compounded to make a kind of family charter or constitution. Either way, it should thoroughly explain the above elements, starting with the rules of interaction.

The first step when logging the rules of interaction among family members is to establish a form of family governance. For smaller families – those with first generation wealth – the ruling body is usually the two parents who hold all of the family assets. For larger families, things are naturally more complex. It may be in the best interest of both the business and the family to elect various members of the family to serve on a council that determines the rules and regulations that all family members must follow. It is always best to include a representative from each generation of the family – this way, all members, whatever their age, have a voice in the proceedings.

These councils can be structured like a typical financial or governmental body. They should be composed of a broad range of family members and should meet regularly. During the early meetings, the council could determine when and where all future meetings should take place and assign responsibilities to each family member. The structure is simple, just like any organization. There could be a president, vice president, secretary, and a treasurer (as needed). Document rules and regulations for all family members to follow both during and free from council meetings, and, finally, draft methods and demands for each council member to gather information and report back to the council as a whole.

Having a "ruling body" such as this creates a respectable structure within the family. It takes the heat off of the sole owner and delegates it among the council members. Of course, just like the mission statement, the council must be flexible and adaptable. It too must change with the times. If the family changes and the council, with its rules and regulations, does not, the communication and values that it commands tend to break down. Conflict arises.

The next category of interest that the mission statement or family constitution could cover is a decree of the family's basic value system. It is impossible to compile a comprehensive statement of family values without everyone having a working knowledge of what brought the family to its current state in the first place. Drafting an overarching history of the family can be a time-consuming task, but it is absolutely necessary if one wants to have an accurate grasp of the key value structures of the family as a whole. This history must include a brief biography of ancestors, a detailed story of the founding of the family business – along with key steps and trends that brought the business to its successful state – and a complete outline of the values and influences of the family as it is today. Tools for gathering data for this assignment are revealed later in this segment.

Not only is this history important to the mission statement, it will prove to be an important centerpiece to the family itself. Each member of the family will take pride in the documentation of its ancestors and achievements – and they will all take comfort in knowing that their own history, their own legacy, will live on long after their death.

The next key point of the family mission statement is perhaps the most important. In order to both craft the family mission and ensure that it is carried out, opening the lines of communication among family members is absolutely essential. Again, communication is very different for first generation families of wealth and families that span across many generations. For the former, communication can begin, and find a great deal of success, just at the dinner table. The more the parents discuss the family values and goals at the dinner table, the more likely the children will comfortably grow into roles of greater leadership. For multigenerational families, however, communication is naturally a more complex issue. Families with many branches that span across the globe may have to exert greater effort in order to ensure that the lines of communication stay open. Some effective methods include retreats or reunions. More on this subject later in this segment.

The bottom line is that communication is extremely valuable to any decision making process. Allowing for everyone to voice their opinion is an effective way to foster cohesion within the family unit. When determining your successor, for example, more of your family members are likely to agree with your decision if they feel like they have had a say in the matter, even if your decision does not reflect (or even contradicts) their own opinions.

The final task for the family mission or constitution is to provide a summary of the three essential categories of goals that the family maintains. The essential categories can be divided as follows: Financial goals, intellectual goals, and personal goals. Financial goals are obvious – make enough money to maintain a comfortable lifestyle for this and all future generations. Intellectual and personal goals have greater variance from person to person. Intellectual goals involve a desire to expand one's knowledge about the family or broader, more traditional topics such as science or the arts. The more each family member contributes to building his/her own understanding, the greater the intellectual capital of the family as a whole – assuming, of course, that every member chooses to share the new insights with the rest of the group. And as broad as intellectual goals are, personal goals are even broader. They can range from a yearning to travel the world to a desire to donate a large sum of money to a local charity.

The best way to maintain the focus on these goals is to provide physical representation of their achievement. In addition to enthusiastic family participation and attendance at landmark occasions such as religious rites, graduations, and marriages, celebrating family-specific ceremonies and traditions is an excellent way to display the importance of achieving individual and familial goals. These kinds of actions are central to every tight-knit, successful family. Some families have coming-of-age ceremonies wherein members of the youngest generation, upon reaching a certain age, are granted access to a greater understanding of the family and its business. This passage into adulthood can be symbolized with a specific ritual or heirloom – such as the presentation of the family crest.

Having all of these elements – goals, values, history, and rules – serves as a springboard for success for the family. It gives a viewpoint to drive efforts and actions. It builds unity and pride.

Now that we've outlined the significance of the family mission statement and all of its components, we must shift focus and reveal the best methods for compiling all of the necessary data.

Obviously, in any family that surrounds a specific business, the first and most important historical facts to amass have to do with the business itself. In order for this and all future generations to make the best decisions about the fate of the family business, they must first come to an understanding and appreciation for its founding, its founder – along with all subsequent leaders – and all of the turning points that it has endured over the years. For most, this is a fairly easy history to record: after all, unless your name is Rockefeller, Carnegie, or Hearst, your family business has probably not been around for more than one or two generations.

Since the business is defined by its relationship to the family, the next history to be compiled is that of each family member. Traditional methods such as building family trees and interviewing the eldest kin are still highly effective. Another interesting – and more contemporary – method, however, is that of photojournalism. Virtual histories have grown in popularity over the past several years. Those without a basic understanding of current technology can hire a third-party representative to videotape interviews of any and all family members necessary to create a comprehensive history of the family itself. Once it is digital, the family history can be stored, enjoyed, and expanded whenever needed. Copies can be made for everyone – and even the youngest generations can enjoy learning about their ancestors. The eldest members of the family can take comfort in knowing that theirs and the family's legacy will live on in digital format for many generations to come. Think of it as a living, user friendly, family library.

Shifting away from the topic of history, we have already mentioned the importance of assessing the individual values and goals of each family member. This action is absolutely essential to crafting an all-encompassing family mission statement or constitution – along with some of the other key elements to building family harmony that we have not yet discussed. Gathering this type of data is fairly simple. The most effective method to employ involves drafting a series of questionnaires or "value-assessment cards" to be distributed to each member of the family. To illustrate the types of questions that need to be asked, we provide the sample on the following page:

Stevenson Family Value-Assessment Questionnaire

Name:

Age:

Parents' Names:

Goal Assessment

Where do you see yourself in ten years?

List at least three of your aspirations in life:

What steps need to be taken in order for you to reach these aspirations?

Do you have any goals that are specifically related to either the family or the family business? If so, what are they?

Value Assessment

List the following disciplines in the order of their importance to you:

___ Money

___ Family

___ Intellectual Advancement

___ Integrity

___ Reputation

___ Religion

___ Philosophy

In three sentences or less, write a personal mission statement:

If charged with the task of writing a mission statement for the family, what kinds of values would you want to include?

How important is the family business to you?

If you were offered a meaningful role within the family business, would you take it? What would it mean to you?

The questionnaire that you choose to employ could be as in-depth as you desire. Questions can be as general as those provided above or as specific as "If I considered you to be a capable successor to my role as owner of the family business, would you be willing to take over when I retire?" or "Which member of the family, in your opinion, would be a capable successor to my role as owner of the family business?" Whatever the case, the more people who provide answers to your questions, the better. Having access to the goals and values of each member of the family is the best way to ensure that your mission statement or constitution appeals to everyone involved – and, to be certain, if the family mission statement doesn't appeal to everyone involved, then sitting down to write it was little more than a waste of time. If anyone within the family has reason to object to any point included in the mission statement, it will not serve as the effective method to achieving family cohesion, as we have advertised. In fact, it will be just the opposite – a cause for dispute rather than a call to unity.

Once the family mission has been conceived, your family has taken the first of many steps to ensure success throughout future generations. A family mission statement is a nice piece to hang on the wall of your home or office, but it means nothing unless it is put into practice. The family must be willing to adopt clear-cut rules that establish proper interaction among the group and decision making skills regarding both business and pleasure. Each family member must have both a say in the creation of the rules and a responsibility to enforce them. Full representation is critical because the real danger here is having the generation currently in control of the family business impose their will on the next.

Century Plan

Full participation on the part of each family member on the rules and regulations to govern the family requires a documented understanding of the family focus, philosophy, strategy. If it is allowed to constantly evolve, this picture can be projected out through vast amounts of time – a veritable century plan. In fact, let's refer to it as the "Century Plan". That's not a bad title.

A working Century Plan can be structured however the family sees fit, but the most effective contain rules for governance of three key disciplines. The family must first come to an understanding of acceptable family values and behavior. Next, the interaction between the family and the business – along with the wealth that it generates – must be discussed. And, finally, the family must be informed of its relationship to the surrounding community. Everyone needs to understand what is and is not considered acceptable behavior both inside and outside the family setting.

Taking the concept of the Century Plan even further, the goal-related data that you have collected from each member of your family can be used to structure a far-reaching goal structure. Listed in the Century Plan should be the family aspirations for the growth of the business, the gelling of the family, the personal and intellectual improvement of each individual according to his/her own interests and belief structures, and a well-documented position on the importance of giving back to the community. The first and second important goal structures are fairly obvious. The goal of every business is to grow in wealth and the goal of every family should be to grow in love and spirit.

The third important goal perhaps deserves a bit more elaboration. It is critical that each member of the family be allowed to learn and develop according to his/her own interests. Otherwise, what ends up happening is – as previously alluded to – the elder generation ends up imposing its will on the younger. Resentment ensues. Bonds break down. Remember, no matter what the interests of your children – financial pursuits, religion, politics, art, however tedious the potential topics may seem to you – the betterment of them tends to directly contribute to the betterment of the group. For example, perhaps the most intelligent thing that John D. Rockefeller Sr. did – besides turning Standard Oil into an American corporate juggernaut – was to allow John Jr. to pursue other interests. Sr.

had spent several years conditioning his son to be his successor. However, shortly following the revelation of a scandal involving a Standard Oil executive, Jr. had an epiphany. He realized that his life calling was philanthropy. Sr., fortunately for the company as well as the Rockefeller name, had enough foresight to understand that Jr.'s pursuits would be better spent within the arena of his choice. With a heavy heart, John D. Rockefeller Sr. granted his son the permission to follow his own dreams. The rest is history: Jr. went on to spearhead the family's much renowned charitable efforts. The Rockefeller name – not to mention New York City – would not be what it is today if John D. Jr. had not provided such an overwhelming cultural influence through his efforts in charity.

This leads us to our last goal structure – the significance of which is also often underemphasized. Sure, most people of wealth have a tendency to give back to the surrounding communities – but whether this is a guilt-driven motivation or just some appeal to a greater sense of good is unclear. Whatever the case, let it be known that philanthropic goals are every bit as important as generating wealth – and often lead to a better community reputation for both your family and your business, helping both to maintain success and stability well into the future.

Like the family mission statement, the Century Plan takes a great deal of effort and support from every member of the family. But yours is scattered throughout the globe, you say? Getting everyone together to agree on anything seems practically impossible? Nonsense. This brings us to our next – and final – issue associated with family communications: The (at least) annual family meeting.

The Family Meeting

Assembling a large multigenerational family can seem like a logistical nightmare – especially when considering the fact that most large families, when brought together, tend to rear the ugly head of social dysfunction. Trying though it is, calling upon each member of your family to attend an annual family meeting is absolutely essential to the welfare of both the business and the family itself.

Here's why it's significant: We have spent many several pages outlining the importance of gathering data and completing mission statements and broad-based strategies, but we have not yet explained the venue in which to do so. This is it. This is also the venue in which to teach younger generations the importance of the aforementioned principles, the significance of the family history, and the reverence for both personal and communal causes. What's more, a fulfilling and well-organized family meeting has a way of promoting the established family vision or purpose. It unites the most distant of kin – and prevents even the globally-dispersed families from becoming complacent within their own divided groups and alienating themselves from the other branches of the "tree."

Here's where you have it: Neutral ground! We can't stress that enough. Inviting your extended family into your home for run-of-the-mill luncheons – following it up with a trip to the company board room for a dry speech on the quarterly outlook – is sure to be met with an unfavorable response. You can be sure that the turnout will not be quite what it would be if you'd decided to hold it in Las Vegas, for example. Not that Vegas is necessarily the best answer either. The best place to hold a family meeting, perhaps – assuming it is affordable for everyone involved – is an all-inclusive, family oriented resort. Two to three days is all that is necessary. And this type of environment allows for the family to focus on the missions of the meeting while simultaneously taking time to rest and recuperate from the rigors of daily life.

Here's the first problem that most people have with this concept: Every family enjoys a highly-eclectic set of individual personalities. "Enjoys" is maybe not the best word. "Endures" or "suffers" is perhaps a better assessment of the situation. Every family is a hodgepodge of conflicting personalities – conservatives and bleeding-heart liberals, industrialists and environmentalists, narcissists and self-deprecators; all jostling, interacting, and arguing to no end. Bringing all of these people into the same world-class resort, much less the same room, may seem like a veritable impossibility.

Here's the solution: Hire a mediator. An excellent mediator is well-qualified to handle heated social situations – this usually means having a degree or background in family (or even clinical) psychiatry. If there are particular members of your family that have held long-term grudges against one another – and whose family doesn't have at least two people like this? – then a quality third-party mediator will be sure to do interviews of each family member prior to the meeting. During the interview, the mediator will establish the reasoning behind each point of contention and highlight all of the issues that need to be resolved during the family meeting. Bringing in an outside party has a way of both providing objective opinion to resolve conflict and calming the nerves of even the most irritable of relatives. Most people, after all, are less willing to throw fits or cause a scene if there is an outside observer involved in the discussion.

Here's the three-part general structure: the business meeting, the educational program, and the social events (i.e. the obligatory fun). The three-part general structure meets the three-pronged objectives to the successful family meeting. The goal is to discuss the business, advance everyone's understanding of business and societal goals, and strengthen family ties.

The first item on the agenda should be the business meeting. Financial and legal documents can be prepared for review before the meeting takes place. Once on site, those in the family who have reached the U.S.-standard age of intellectual enlightenment (18) and desire to take part in determining the direction of the family business, should be allowed to attend the meeting. Obviously, this standard isn't absolute. Basically, anyone, young or old, whom you think could add special insight to the meeting should be invited.

If a mediator has been hired, the first step is to lay out the rules governing behavior and interaction. Families with especially excitable relatives can go as far as to set regulations against the raising of voices, abrupt and aggravated exits, the throwing of objects or slamming of doors. Whatever necessary. Once this has been established, the focus can shift to such issues as estate planning, quarterly financial performance, charitable giving, or – and we're especially fond of this particular topic – succession planning. Where necessary, the family can invite financial advisors or accountants to provide a professional opinion on the economic outlook of the business. The bottom line is that the level of formality during this portion of the family meeting is entirely up to you and the participating members. It can be seen as a way to comprehensively forecast the future direction of the business or just a method to update everyone on the progress you have made over the past year.

The second portion of the family meeting is the educational program. The natural reaction is to associate education with youth. During the family meeting this is not entirely the case. While it is important to provide programs to teach the youngest generation about money management and family values – these traits aren't genetically inherited, after all – it is equally important to hold seminars wherein the elder generations learn about topics such as improving the quality of leadership, market trends, or relevant financial strategies. With this dual-layered educational program, the elder generations learn how to become more effective leaders while the younger generations simultaneously learn to follow in the footsteps of their parents and grandparents. The result is a more knowledgeable family – one with a working understanding of the roles that each member plays; creating a heightened sense of respect and togetherness.

Materials for the educational programs can range from a seminar-like presentation and breakout session model – complete with a qualified and engaging keynote speaker – to mock business leadership scenarios. Both distant listening and hands-on interaction are effective ways to relay a message. Different people and learning capacities demand different methods of education. It is important that, whatever types of educational materials or strategies you prefer, your curriculum is eclectic enough to meet this fundamental need.

This brings us to the final point of both the family meeting portion and the chapter as a whole: the time to unwind. Whenever asked to participate in a high-intensity educational or professional program, one must be allowed a little time to blow off steam. This is especially true considering the fact that the family meeting requires us to break out of our usual familial relationships and pretend to be almost like coworkers for large blocks of time. In order to combat this kind of discomfort, you must provide your family members with the occasion to have fun with one another. This is exactly why an all-inclusive resort is the best place to hold the family meeting. Once the formality of the work day is left behind, your relatives must be allowed to golf, swim, play tennis, shop, or do whatever strikes their fancy – as long as it is in good spirits and with one another, building familial bonds. Set up games or competitions. Provide outings. Have a good time. Though it is intended for the betterment of the family business, this is perhaps the true essence of the family meeting: Enjoying the environment, relaxation, kinship, and oneself.

We've said a lot in this chapter, we know. It is important to understand that all of it works hand in hand. If you have reason to be concerned about the way your family will react to your succession planning, schedule a family meeting. Contact a resort to book a reservation. Work closely with your family members on building a mission statement, creed, or constitution. Distribute questionnaires and take steps to compile a family history. Work, consult, and play together. You will leave the meeting with a greater sense of confidence in your decisions; your family will too.

Chapter 5

Asset Protection

For those that doubt the necessity of asset protection, consider the fact that the United States employs more than 90% of the world's lawyers.

It's a startling thought – and you can enter your own lawyer joke here – but the result is shaky ground for any individual of high net-worth. In the arena of civil law, the proverbial scales of justice of the United States judicial system are often grossly over-weighted in favor of the plaintiff. This, coupled with the fact that the U.S. is one of the only countries in the world that allows lawyers to be paid a contingency fee for carrying out a successful lawsuit, makes for a rather cutthroat legal playing field. Some statistics suggest that there is a new lawsuit filed in the U.S. every thirty seconds. But what types of people should be concerned about asset protection? And how can the average American protect him/herself against the storm? We're glad you asked.

Who Should Be Concerned about Asset Protection?

All high-net-worth individuals, whether the wealth was earned or inherited, members of public company boards, owners of expansive residential or commercial real estate, and any wealthy individuals in high-risk occupations, specifically physicians and successful business owners, should consider the prospect of asset protection. Simply put, anyone of high income and high tax bracket status should find interest in the following strategies.

Anyone at risk of being pursued by creditors or working in a profession that exposes them to malpractice or other lawsuits – and especially those working busy schedules with no time to manage their personal finances or those lacking sufficient access to information – should seek the assistance of a financial advisor.

In the United States, anyone with a net-worth of over $50,000 is three times as likely to be sued. If you have reason to fear this statistic, it would certainly be in your interest to protect yourself and your financial future.

In the interest of precision, the following is a list of people who specifically need to be concerned about asset protection:

- High-Risk Medical Professionals – Surgeons, anesthesiologists and oncologists may regularly be involved in emotionally charged medical events. This exposure, coupled with the perception of physicians as wealthy individuals, can galvanize an attack.

- Business Owners – Your office space and your status as employer can make you the target of disgruntled employees and/or visitors to your office or plant site. Even when there is no obvious fault or negligence on your part, a lawsuit may be pursued in the hopes of tapping your perceived "deep pockets." After over 100 years of labor/management disputes in the United States, the role of "owner" can charge extremely negative emotions – regardless of your reputation for generosity and fairness.

- Property Owners – Insurance may not fully protect you from residents and visitors who are injured on your property or who experience an illness or become a victim of crime while visiting one of your properties. The larger your holdings, the wider your exposure and the more attractive you become as a target.

- Senior Executives and Board Members of Corporations – In recent years, because of a growing number of highly publicized leadership failings, executives and board members are becoming targets of "get even" litigations. As in all such cases, the larger the pool of assets, the more attractive you are to the potential litigators.

- Family Money and Inheritances – "Found" money such as this can stir deep feelings of jealousy and resentment. Whenever such feelings are combined with personal need there is a potential for attack.

If you fall under one of these categories – and if you're reading this book, you most certainly fall under at least the second category – we know you'll be interested in the following key strategies for ensuring that expensive and time-consuming lawsuits never manage to debilitate you or your business.

6 Strategies for Protecting Your Assets

Strategy One: Investment Oriented Insurance Products

Specifically, the products referred to in this section are annuities and life insurance. These products can be viewed as a tax-strategy with benefits. In many cases, the insurance policy also protects the holder from the losses associated with lawsuits. Furthermore, the policy may ensure a smoother transition of assets in the event of death. The proceeds from a life insurance or annuity policy can be transferred to beneficiaries while avoiding the often-difficult probate process. Heirs can choose between receiving a deferred payout or a lump sum payment – all the while ducking the expenses and delay of the probate process.

Any money included in a *fixed annuity* accrues interest just as with any bank account or CD only this type of policy has a twist. Think of a fixed annuity as an investment sans the hassle of having to pay taxes on its earnings. With credited interest on the part of the insurance company, taxes are only paid when the holder decides to begin making withdrawals or receive an annuity income. Since it is tax-deferred, a fixed annuity has the potential to accumulate greater value in a shorter period of time – vastly improving the holder's financial situation.

A fixed annuity also offers a sense of security. A life insurance company must provide reserves equivalent to the withdrawal value of the annuity. These reserves are a kind of financial obligation that a life insurance company must meet in order to protect the money invested by the holder. By law in many states, a life insurance company must also provide a given level of capital and surplus in addition to reserves – further protecting the holder's assets.

A *variable annuity* functions much in the same way as a fixed annuity, only it carries with it a greater level of risk. The risk associated with the variable annuity may involve participation in the stock or bond markets. Obviously, just like any other market-oriented investment, a variable annuity faces the possibility of decreasing in value

Perhaps the most attractive aspect of variable annuities is flexibility. The holder can transfer money from one sub-account to another – within the annuity – without the penalty of taxes. This allows the holder to accommodate for changing market conditions without current tax consequences.

Strategy Two: Life Insurance

Life insurance has many of the same advantages as annuities including tax deferral, avoidance of probate, and being a vehicle for potential asset protection. There are also fixed and variable forms that allow for customization to fit the demands of a particular situation. Of course, life insurance also provides enhanced liquidity at the inevitable death of the insured. Purchasing specific types of life insurance products allows you to provide significant resources to children, grandchildren or philanthropic interests after your death. By investing assets in a life insurance policy you effectively send a gift forward in time to the person or persons for which you wish to provide, and eliminate those assets from potential discovery during your lifetime. The life insurance contract functions in a way quite similar to the annuity product, in that it shields those assets from attack while allowing you to control the assets for your purposes.

Your insurance broker can provide access to various life insurance and annuity products; however, it is prudent to consult with your investment advisor about how these products can best be deployed as part of a larger, asset protection strategy. Before using any specific strategy, you may wish to pursue a comprehensive planning process with a qualified financial advisor who specializes in asset protection strategies for high net-worth clients. An effective strategy will usually involve the use of several investment vehicles and legal actions to provide comprehensive and strategic protection.

Strategy Three: Offshore Investing

Disclaimer: This is a highly specialized approach that may not be for everyone. You need to consider offshore investing very carefully – and it should only be adopted under the guidance of expert advice.

For business owners or other individuals in high-risk professions, offshore investing may be a sophisticated way to protect and privatize assets. While some may fear that any money held in a distant proximity may be more difficult and costly to manage, the fact remains that offshore investing may provide the most comfortable blanket against asset-damaging litigation.

Creating an offshore trust is simply the act of investing money in a bank outside of the legal jurisdiction of the United States. The reason that this act is so appealing is that banks in many countries enjoy more protection from creditors than we do here in the US. In fact, trusts opened in the US – assuming that the party doing the opening serves as trustee and main beneficiary – do not promise any kind of protection against creditors or litigation. This is simply not true in many other countries. All assets held in foreign lands are free from lawsuits because the country in which they are held simply will not honor the judgments passed on American soil. This is the main reason that, in recent years, offshore investing has grown so rapidly in popularity.

Talk to your attorney or financial advisor to find out how these opportunities can best suit you.

As noted, this option isn't for everyone. Maintaining and managing money in an offshore account has the tendency to either be expensive to the user or tie up more money than necessary. Unless you are at extremely high risk for lawsuits, offshore investing may not be the right strategy for you.

Strategy Four: Asset Protection Trusts

Another option when pursuing offshore investing is the Asset Protection Trust – an option so attractive in defending oneself against lawsuits that even a lawyer may wish to jump on the bandwagon. This type of trust is very similar to a standard domestic trust. The settler transfers all of the assets into the trust, which is controlled largely by a trustee – typically, although not in every case, the trustee is a foreign trust company that operates outside of the United States. This provides a shield from U.S. legislation – taking advantage of the stricter privacy laws that exist in most other parts of the world. Like most trusts, this arrangement allows the trustees to distribute income to the beneficiaries – among these beneficiaries may be the settler and his/her spouse, children, and grandchildren. The timeframe for the trust may be as little as a few years or could extend even beyond the settler's death.

The aspect of the asset protection trust that makes it unique, however, is that it also carries a "protector." The protector, appointed by the settler, oversees the action of the trustees. None of the settler's assets may be moved without the consent of the appointed protector.

Essentially, the major attraction to this method is that asset protection trusts remove the settler's assets from his/her estate, rendering them inaccessible to creditors – through the precedent known as the spendthrift clause. This clause allows the settler to keep his/her assets, while technically removing them from his/her estate. As previously mentioned, this action usually crosses overseas; however, four states have now enacted legislation authorizing self-settled spendthrift trusts. These states are Alaska, Delaware, Nevada, and Rhode Island.

Strategy Five: Exemption Planning

Exemption planning is also a key ingredient to asset protection. Exempt assets can include a home, pension plan, personal wages, the previously mentioned annuities and life insurance, household goods, and vehicles, among others. Many of these categories have dollar caps that vary from state to state, so it is important to consult a lawyer or financial advisor regarding how beneficial this strategy may be for you.

The first key element to this planning is a *Homestead Exemption*. This secures a personal residence from most creditors' claims. Again, the exemption standards vary from state to state. Some states such as Florida and Texas provide an unlimited cap. In order to exploit the exemption the most effectively, an individual should take careful consideration of these standards. If the state's homestead exemption is unlimited or the amount of the potential exemption is greater than the value of the home, the individual should pay off the mortgages on the property. On the other hand, if the value of the home is greater than the state's exemption cap, the individual should consider increasing the mortgage. If the state carries little or no homestead exemption, then the individual should consider owning the home with a spouse in "tenancy by the entirety" – taking the home out of the reach of the creditors of either individual because the action legally binds the married couple into one entity. This last strategy is only effective if the individual has no reason to fear divorce.

Assets held in a retirement account may also provide a high degree of protection from creditors. This could include IRAs (Roth and traditional), Simple plans, 401(k) assets, 403(b) plans, defined benefit plans, and others. It is important to note, however, that in many states, in order to avoid a lawsuit against an IRA, the carrier may have to file for bankruptcy. Since this is the case, many people keep most of their money in their 401(k) at work, since they are exempt from lawsuits. Money can always be rolled into an IRA later, anyway. This may seem like a fraudulent conveyance, but it is entirely legal and practiced by many.

Tools of the Trade and *Personal Property Exemption* may serve as two other viable strategies. Valuable personal goods can be considered exempt property. Tools of the trade may also be considered exempt and can carry broad terms. Generally, if used to carry out a business process, it is a tool of the trade. If a personal vehicle is frequently used to run errands for a business, for example, it may also be added to the exempt category.

Strategy Six: Using the Corporate Shield

"Using the Corporate Shield" is a relatively simple strategy for protecting one's assets. Essentially, in order to "shield" personal assets from liability claims, an individual may set up a corporation. Legally speaking, the corporation is a separate entity. Assets may be transferred into the name of the corporation.

One example of a corporation is a Limited Liability Company (LLC). Setting up an LLC provides protection from an individual's liability, but does not establish a company in the literal sense. This type of company is simply a separate entity and not exposed to the formalities of shareholders, bylaws, and corporate directors – because a typical company with these characteristics may be exposed to lawsuits against individual shareholders or officers. Lawsuits against members of an LLC are often prohibited.

An LLC also does not pay income tax because it is legally viewed as a kind of partnership as opposed to a corporation. All income and deductions are reported on the owners' income tax returns. This affords the owners a little flexibility concerning administration and operation issues.

An owner's name does not necessarily have to be disclosed. Many states, such as Nevada, Delaware, and Rhode Island, permit an LLC to be formed anonymously by a single person. This creates an environment of financial privacy – including, but not restricted to, anonymous financial accounts and real estate.

Unfortunately, not all business owners are eligible for this strategy. Legislation has not yet allowed physicians or other individuals exposed to the potential for malpractice suits to open an LLC.

Strategy Seven: Applying Common Sense

This section may seem trivial, but never underestimate good old-fashioned common sense. Sometimes what seems obvious or taken for granted is exactly what we forget to consider. So, read on. You might find something that surprises you.

- First and foremost, in the above sections, we have provided you with all of these ways to avoid lawsuits – but what happens when one slips through the cracks? Never ignore a lawsuit. Ever. It is important to get high-quality advice from a lawyer that you trust.

- Keep your insurance. Even the most tightly knit asset protection plan can be vulnerable. Adequate insurance will still be necessary to serve as the safety net. Oftentimes, the greatest value of the insurance policy is overlooked: the insurance company must provide you with a defense.

- Avoid the hearty handshake agreement – and all other vague or general partnerships. Any and all general partners are liable for a company's actions. Be careful when selecting colleagues.

- Get good advice. Talk to a financial planner about all assets. Talk to a lawyer – preferably a local lawyer in whom you trust – before making any large moves. The lawyer may be able to negotiate fees or point out loopholes that would have been overlooked otherwise.

- Be stealthy. It may seem like a military term, but it applies to the business world as well. Essentially, this means that you should avoid putting everything in your own name. Never under any circumstances should you show off your wealth. The richer you appear, the more likely you are to get sued. This does not mean that you have to live a modest lifestyle, just keep a low profile.

- Consider purchasing risk-management consultations for your business and personal properties. Many insurance companies will provide some risk-management consultation; and will be able to refer you to appropriate professional consultants for more advanced assessments. Retain all records of risk-management assessments, and fulfill the recommendations that are made.

- Pay attention to state law. Again, talk to your lawyer. Some states are more liberal than others. This may serve in your favor.

- Be careful when selecting colleagues and business partners. Put all relationships into formal, legal agreements that include remedies and define the limits of liabilities of each party. Never assume to predict the future behavior of another person, regardless of how close you may feel to them today. Relationships change and people can become desperate or irrationally angry in unpredictable ways.

7 Simple Steps to Protecting Your Wealth

The first step in more fully protecting your assets from litigation and attack is to become educated about the obvious and not-so-obvious strategies that are available to you. Given the growing potential for litigation attack, education alone is not enough. Most business owners are caught off guard by unexpected lawsuits. If you have not erected a comprehensive strategy well before a litigation is begun, it is too late.

There are 7 simple steps that you can take to protect your wealth from outside attack:

Step One: Take the risk to your wealth seriously. Set a specific calendar goal by which you plan to have a comprehensive asset protection plan in place. Budget the time necessary each week over the next few months to achieve this plan.

Step Two: Assemble a team of advisors. Your team should include a skilled tax attorney, estate attorney, and trust attorney. Many larger law firms that specialize in serving high net-worth clients will have specialists available on their staff to advise you. Your team should also include a CPA and a qualified financial advisor who has specialized in working with high net-worth clients and in the creation of asset protection plans. Your financial advisor may also work for a firm that makes offshore investing available to clients. Without this strategy your plan will likely miss a vital dimension of protection.

Step Three: Review your estate plans, current investment plans, your business succession plans, and philanthropic goals. Your team will need a clear picture of your total financial structure, your intentions, and your preferences. Expect to invest a substantial amount of time clarifying both your current situation and your future intentions.

Step Four: Conduct a comprehensive risk assessment consultation of your personal and business holdings, and provide this assessment to your team. Your risk analysis should include attention to your current insurance coverage and various obvious and not-so-obvious exposures to risk.

Step Five: Request that your team builds a comprehensive, written plan that incorporates all of the specific expertise you have assembled to advise you. Review the plan fully and become thoroughly educated about the various aspects and processes involved. Make sure you understand the limits on access and liquidity of each part of the strategy.

Step Six: Implement! In spite of the time, effort and energy that will be required and the necessary expenses involved in executing some of the strategies, a plan not implemented is useless. Protecting your wealth requires a balancing act between distancing yourself from your assets and controlling your assets. Learning how to control your wealth at a distance may be the hardest part of this transition.

Step Seven: Change your behaviors. Think of yourself as a potential target and avoid actions that may call undue attention to your wealth. You live in a highly litigious society and, as a person of high net-worth, you have joined the dubious club of "deep pocket" targets. By building a comprehensive asset protection plan and resolving to mount a vigorous, even aggressive, response to potential litigation, you will discourage future attacks on your prosperity and security.

All of these strategies and steps are effective in their own way. All business practitioners are unique. The business world is ever-changing – and the legal world will continue to encroach.

Hopefully, we have shown you that there is still hope. Find an excellent advisor and an excellent lawyer, apply a few of these strategies, and you will be well on your way to quieting the storm.

Section 3:
Employee and Executive Relations

Chapter 6

Selecting Your Successor

Perhaps you've been at the reins for several decades now. If you want your legacy to last, you must face the task of picking and training the right person or persons to serve as your successor. Since this is a family-oriented book, we'll focus on the assumption that your successor will be from within the family. More often than not, this person is a son or daughter (or son- or daughter-in-law), but is he/she the right man/woman for the job? And if this person already works for you, who will fill the position that he/she vacates? Power transfer often leads to the proverbial domino effect.

While it may seem like a rather elementary concept, many business owners fail to plan for this monumental event. Instead they simply select a successor, wish him/her luck, and motor off, leaving a very large vacuum in their wake.

The reverse is also true (and just as likely and every bit as problematic). Many business owners simply lack the capacity to give up something that they've put so much of themselves into over the course of all these years. Who could blame them? A great deal of sweat and tears and triumphs must be left behind – and that is never easy.

The first and most important question to ask yourself before even considering whom you're going to line up as your successor is: Am I willing to let go? While the tone of most business transitions is almost entirely professional, there is always an element of the emotional mixed in. Your particular situation – being in business with family – takes that emotion and amps it up a few levels. Don't kid yourself. Doing what you now intend to do is extremely difficult.

In response to this difficulty, allow us to kick off this chapter by introducing a very small checklist that looks much simpler than it really is. From there, we will proceed to explain how you go about completing the tasks. The task of actually checking the boxes, we'll leave to you.

The Training-Your-Successor-Brand Checklist

- ❏ I am ready and willing to let go.
- ❏ I have established an exit strategy.
- ❏ I promise to stick to that strategy.
- ❏ I have picked the right family member to sell to.
- ❏ My successor wants this job.
- ❏ My successor is willing and able to do this job.
- ❏ I recognize that positions will open up when I depart.
- ❏ All these positions are now filled.
- ❏ I have properly trained everyone for their new roles.

The Family (and/or Personal) Mess

The main reason that businesses fail when passed to the next generation is that their founders simply, and many times foolishly, assume that their children have the desire and talent necessary to take leadership in stride. The prospect of the child taking over the family business is presumed and left unsaid. It's related in the will or parting agreement as though by afterthought. The result is a child who is uninformed, improperly trained, and often unwilling to run the business.

The second reason that businesses fail when passed to the next generation works hand-in-hand with the first: your sons or daughters may be completely uninterested in owning a business. Regardless of what your business means to you and the family as a whole, it is a fair bet that your offspring will have other aspirations in life. There is an old adage that the parents study war and politics so that their children can study finance and management and their children's children can study sculpture, painting, and music. If you've managed your business so effectively that your family has achieved a level of great affluence, there is a good chance that your children have been raised in an environment that influenced them to pursue other interests.

So what if you don't have any children wanting to take the helm? There are plenty of other interested family members, right? Right. This actually creates another problem: there may be too many interested family members. If you've ever coordinated a family reunion, wedding, or large scale graduation party, you probably realize that getting a consensus among family members is pretty much equivalent to herding cats. Who do you choose as a successor? How much control does the family maintain? Will the in-laws be properly compensated? What of the children – by heavens, think of the children! Without advanced planning, expect these frantic and heated questions.

Since it is so hard to imagine a relatively pain-free succession – and since most are so in love with their work that they can't imagine getting up in the morning just to play golf – many business owners stick around, running things for far too long. This is problematic because, sometimes, with age comes complacency. Sometimes, with age comes uncertainty. These factors combine to create an aging business owner that both doubts the prospect of his/her family business succeeding under new management and fears the prospect of running out of money at any point during the retirement. Most business owners do not realize that every business reaches a critical point where it either changes management or dies. If the only reason that you are still in control of your business is so you can compile a large enough nest egg to last you the rest of your natural days, then for the sake of your business, your family, and yourself, it may be time to plan your succession. The crucial and sometimes painful step of this process is choosing the right heir to your office chair.

Selecting a Successful Successor (Say that three times fast)

1. Which member of my family is qualified to handle the responsibility of managing my business after I depart?

2. How do I leave the business to one of my children and be sure that I'm treating the others fairly?

Because of the complexity and difficulty of Question #1, many owners avoid it altogether. Coldly assessing the strengths and weaknesses of one's children can be a painful task. However, it is vital to the continued success of your business. After all, running a business is hard work – it takes a lot of creative thinking – and not everyone is qualified to fill such large shoes. The bottom line is that there really is no way to guarantee that you've chosen the correct successor. Assessing the leadership strengths and weaknesses of a person who may never have been in a leadership role before is not easy. The logistics are just plain messy. There are strategies, by no means fool-proof, but strategies we will provide.

Regarding Question #2, most parents don't like to play favorites among their children. Even though one child might be clearly the most qualified to take over in your stead, it is very difficult, upon retirement, to leave the others with nothing. Many business owners opt for the most obvious solution: just divide controlling interest equally among all of the children. This may seem like a just move, at first – and perhaps it *is* the most just way to go – however, it can be extremely detrimental to the health of your business. There are outside factors to consider. These factors include in-laws and other familial influences that tend to fly under the radar until control has been passed from your hands. Even ignoring all of that, you must understand that leaving a business to the shared control of people who argued about the shared control of new toys as young children can be a highly volatile matter. Conflict is likely to ensue – and conflict is exactly the kind of poison to bring even the most stable of family businesses crashing down. If you are considering the prospect of carving up control of the family business, please remember: *Fair does not always mean equal and equal does not always mean fair.*

In Answer to Question #1

Assessing Interest

Assessing interest on the part of the successor is such a simple step to every succession plan – and, yet, it is so often overlooked or altogether ignored. Our first and most concrete solution is that, in order to assess interest, you must *talk to your children.* Never (ever) assume that, just because your business means the world to you, it will mean the world to your first born child. Everyone has different interests – and, unless you open the lines of communication with your children, you may never discover which of them (if any) can devote his/her best efforts to keeping the family business alive.

How you choose to open the lines of communication is entirely up to you. It can be handled formally, in a well-planned and structured meeting with all of your children. Hold it in the company conference room, provide direct presentation, numbers, facts, and figures, and see whose interest peaks. Or it can be handled informally. Call each of your children on the phone and simply ask them if they've thought about or even counted on taking over in your stead. If direct contact isn't really your style, assessing interest can be effectively confined to paper. Provide each of your children with a questionnaire that outlines their values and desires in life. Be sure to include a question that asks each of your children to rate their pride and respect for the company business and desire to lead it in the future.

Whichever method you choose, it is important to understand that, once you've established which of your children is most interested in the family business, the process is *not*, in fact, over. It never fails: once you announce that you're passing the business on to your successor, his/her siblings – the ones who previously established their complete disinterest in maintaining relative control over the family business – will have a change of heart and demand a piece of the pie. Time and money have a way of changing things. Values and goals are never rock solid. Desires are as unpredictable as the winds. Thus, assessing interest is an ongoing process. Once the lines of communication are opened, they must remain open. Reevaluate your potential successor's interest in the family business on a regular basis.

Assessing Ability

Allow us to flatter you for a moment. You have at least one very special quality – for years, you have demonstrated an ability to complete an incredibly wide range of tasks (and you've obviously done it well). Small business owners must wear any number of hats. Your ability to do so has served you quite well. Your ability to do so is also a very rare quality. Finding a successor (especially if you intend to draw from the smaller pool that is represented by your family) that can meet all of the challenges that you've met over the years should not be taken lightly. It's simply too critical and too difficult to just gloss over.

We're not sure if we're violating copyrights here but, for an example of a successful business transition, look no further than one of America's most classic films (or trilogies, as it were), *The Godfather*. Brando's too old and hefty to continue on with the family business. He's got three sons: One of them an imbecile, one of them a lunatic, and one of them (the youngest) a level-headed, born leader.

Way too many folks follow the centuries-old tradition and leave the power and fortune to the eldest son or daughter. Make no mistake, in today's by-the-second business world, birthrights mean little to nothing. Just because he/she is your eldest son/daughter doesn't mean that he/she can handle even half of your everyday tasks. What's worse is that there is often a vast chasm between performance potential and actual performance. So many sons or daughters (at least in the eyes of the mother or father) seem to fit the role of the Michael Corleone but wind up performing like Fredo. Even if they do seem to be intellectually capable, they may not have any real interest or ability to follow in your footsteps. They may look like Pacino (and our condolences if your daughter looks like Pacino), they may dress like Pacino, they may have gone to Harvard – they may even be able to articulate the most brilliant business ideas that you've ever heard – but none of these things make them qualified leaders.

So, out of the many members of your family that might look the part and act the part, how do you pick the right one for the job? The first (and really the only) rule of thumb is to avoid putting someone in your place that hasn't demonstrated at least a five year track record of success in some kind of leadership role (preferably within your family or organization).

Once you've properly assessed the interest of your children or other potential heirs, you must plan the most effective way to insert them into the business. Obviously, this kind of planning must be laid out well in advance, especially if you hope to adhere to our five-year-track-record rule. We will illustrate this point with a fictional tale of a business owner with three sons. No, it's not *King Lear*; no, it's not *The Godfather*. In fact, let's make one of the potential heirs a woman. Let's call her Wanda Marlowe and her brothers Darren Jr. and Jerome. Their father is Darren Marlowe, Sr.

The year is 1999 and Darren Sr. has been piloting his family's tool and die business for nearly five decades. Though he can't imagine what life without his work will be like, he realizes that it's probably not in the cards for him to continue working all that long into the 21st century. He's clueless in front of a computer, after all, and it's probably time somebody with formal training in online business take over.

And, lo, daughter Wanda just happens to hold an advanced degree in computer science and another in engineering. She boasts a successful track record in a similar industry, but she's never worked directly for Darren Sr. Nevertheless, she's always kept a close eye on the family business. Taking over for her father someday, to her, would be both an honor and a privilege (one that she knows she would expertly take in stride).

While she might seem like the perfect candidate, Darren Sr. can't seem to shake his mind away from tradition. Darren Jr., his namesake, is the eldest of the three children. Darren Jr. has always had a certain spark – a kind of drive that reminds Sr. an awful lot of himself. What better man to take the helm than one who is essentially a carbon copy of the current leader?

Then there's Jerome – the youngest and perhaps the fondest in the eyes of Darren Sr. Jerome has no real leadership record (unless you count the three years he spent as middle linebacker at the State University). While Darren Sr. would be ashamed to admit it (especially out loud), Jerome has always been the one to make his father proudest. The kid could play – and, without that knee injury, probably would have played for a whole lot longer. Alas, poor Jerome has had to spend the prime of his life attempting to keep his own struggling business afloat. There have been successes, to be sure, but, more often than not, Darren Sr. has had to intervene and bail his son's business out of financial trouble.

During the autumn of 1998, Darren Sr. planted the seed that he would soon step down. He invited all three of his children to take positions of leadership within his company, with the idea that sometime in the coming five years, he would determine his successor based upon the potential that each of them showed under his tutelage.

Wanda would start out in managing the company's information. She would head up the budding website project, a monthly newsletter, and any and all marketing efforts that the company may need in the coming years. Darren Jr. (though he had little training in the matter) would start in accounting – mostly because Sr. had always believed it to be the most essential part of managing a business and he had his eldest son earmarked as his successor before even beginning. Jerome would manage shipping – mostly because he was always the most personable of the three children and managing the abnormally large shipping staff was a task that would certainly require a likeable leader (though his organizational skills left much to be desired).

As the years passed, several things became clear to Darren Sr. The first was that Wanda was exceptionally gifted with computers and possessed a great foresight into the future of world business. She had taken a good, old-fashioned American company and launched it into the global arena. What's more, she had done it virtually on her own. She had been given one assistant and really only answered to her father during her tenure. The second revelation was that Darren Jr., much to Sr.'s dismay, had very little interest in running the family business. His work in the accounting department had grown increasingly sluggish and he had become distant, if not almost aloof. The third and final point that Sr. learned was that his youngest son, Jerome, while every bit the people-person that his father had imagined, was completely incapable of keeping orders and destinations straight. Shipping, for the past half-decade had been something just short of a disaster (and in a time when the company was drifting more and more towards the participation in a global economy).

Can you guess who our fictional business leader picked? Wanda. Absolutely. And Wanda, we're sure, will do very well in the position. We're also sure that, since they respect their father so much, Darren Jr. and Jerome will stick around in their jobs for as long as they can take it or for as long as their sister can put up with their shortcomings. This plan seems like a success, right? The answer may surprise you. More often than not, this kind of plan fails. There are many reasons, which we will number on the pages that follow:

1. Darren Sr. failed to assess the true interests of his children.

He simply placed them into the positions that were best suited to the backgrounds of each potential successor. This concept may seem perfect on paper but consider the logistics of it: So many people spend their lives working toward something that they don't even care about (many of them even hold degrees in subjects that they have little interest in or use for). It's a sad fact. A person could spend decades building a resume that had absolutely nothing to do with his/her true interests or intellectual goals. It happens all the time.

So Darren Sr. placed his three children into jobs at which only one of the three truly excelled (and, really, who's to know if Wanda even liked the job she'd been handed?). Doing so set two of the three potential successors up to fail. You can't often succeed in a job you completely loathe.

2. Darren Sr. left his children to fill one specific career track.

Darren Jr. spent five years in a job he couldn't grasp or truly care about. Jerome had been handed a job he simply couldn't handle on his own. The problem with this scenario is that both Jr. and Jerome sport vast amounts of potential in other areas of influence. In fact, despite Jerome's excellent people skills and Jr.'s chip-off-the-old-block status, the two of them might actually have excelled had they simply switched responsibilities. Perhaps Jerome longed to crunch numbers. Perhaps Jr. never felt more at home than when darkening the massive door of a loading dock. What's more, even though Wanda was a true master of her job, she might have been even more useful in another department (perhaps one that had nothing to do with computers – which, though she holds a degree in the infernal machines, she has little interest in their proliferation).

Darren Sr.'s great folly was that he failed to recognize that he didn't get to where he is today by mastering accounting alone or focusing entirely on the marketing of his company. He had to do it all. Why shouldn't he expect his successor(s) to have to do it all, too? Leaving his children to audition through one (and only one) arena of leadership could very well doom his business to failure. What happens when Wanda needs to crunch the numbers? What happens when Wanda is left to coordinate the shipping? What happens when Wanda actually has to deal with people other than her father and her one personal assistant?

3. Darren Sr. didn't embark upon a consistent (if not constant) process of communication and reassessment.

All three of Darren Sr.'s potential successors hated their respective jobs by the third year. All of them felt that they could have been greater assets to the company (and could learn more about what it takes to be a business owner) within one of the other spheres of influence. All of them were (and are) truly interested in taking the torch from their father and carrying it well into the future – perhaps even passing it on to their own children – but they simply felt frustrated, overtaxed, or even under-challenged.

Darren Sr. made the right decision in making the initial assessment of the potential of each of his children (although he didn't survey any of them formally, as we would have suggested). He did the right thing by allowing them all a five year window to prove themselves. Not once during the course of the five year assessment period, however, did Darren Sr. ask himself the following questions:

- How is Jr./Wanda/Jerome doing in his/her/his job right now?
- Is Jr./Wanda/Jerome happy?
- How would Jr./Wanda/Jerome do in a different leadership position than the one he/she/he currently holds?
- Is he/she/he living up to my expectations?

- Is he/she/he keeping up with the requirements of my five year track?
- Has he/she/he demonstrated that he/she/he will be capable of doing my job (and all of the many random tasks that I must take in stride on a daily basis) by the end of the five year track?

Darren Sr. failed to realize that potential has a threefold value and that it's constantly in flux. It incorporates three elements: past potential, current potential, and future potential. All of this says nothing about the threefold value's distant cousin: the unfortunately titled "potential potential" (or, if we can be terribly redundant: an individual's potential ability to demonstrate potential within an alternate career track).

4. Darren Sr. assessed the abilities of his children on his own.

These aren't simply potential successors that Darren Sr. is considering, here. They are his children. He's changed their diapers. He's had a lifetime to develop biases, favoritisms, and pre-conceived notions. Make no mistake, despite how capable Darren Sr. might think he is at the task of removing the father from the business owner/boss, there is nobody in this world more completely incapable of assessing the potential of his children. His vision is simply too clouded by emotion (which, despite our best efforts, can never be completely ignored).

Sr. should have hired an outside and unbiased consultant to oversee the process of training his successor(s). At the very least, this consultant could have warned Darren that none of his children were truly happy with their current leadership positions and that all of them felt they could display more potential within another department.

5.   Darren Sr. assumed that, because he and he alone had
     always led his company, only one man or woman was
     needed to take things over after he left.

You (the reader) and Darren Sr. have at least one thing in
common. You are both cut from a rare stock of the American
worker. You're an uncommon breed – good at everything (or,
at least, close enough to "everything" to succeed in developing
a business from the ground up). Since this kind of ability is so
rare, what are the odds that any one of his children also
possesses it? Heredity may give them an advantage, but it
certainly doesn't give them a guarantee. Leadership ability may
be more nurture than nature and, as long as that can be
assumed, it shouldn't come as a shock that none of Darren Sr.'s
children is completely capable of handling the kinds of tasks
that their father confronts every day. Jerome, for example, had
already demonstrated this fact when he first required his
father's financial aid to pull his own struggling business out of
the fire.

Just because Darren Sr.'s children aren't jacks- (or janes-) of-
all-trades doesn't mean that they don't have their strengths. It
also doesn't mean that their strengths, when combined,
wouldn't outperform the strengths of their father. Nor does it
mean that the three siblings would be incapable of working
harmoniously towards the same goal.

Imagine a different scenario for a moment. What if all three had
excelled in their positions and all three of them were more than
willing (and more than justified) to lay claim to the family
business? To whom does Darren Sr. pass the company without
playing favorites?

In Answer to Question #2

Fair Does Not Always Mean Equal and Equal Does Not Always Mean Fair

It's not just a clever turn of phrase, it is wise advice. "Fair" and "equal" are too often tossed around as simile. It may be difficult to convince your more discerning family members of this fact. Just because one of your kin has been awarded with a shiny new company and the others have been given cash or other property awards does not mean that you haven't handled things fairly. If anything, you may have ensured the family's continued affluence because you've taken the only feasible step towards maintaining the success of your business through future generations.

The first cause for conflict is almost as old as dirt: sibling rivalry. If one of your children is granted control of the family business while the other is gifted a small plot of environmentally protected forest land – or worse, left to maintain his/her position as head of the mailing department in the family company, doomed to be bossed around by his/her younger/older sibling – resentment is likely to boil to the surface. Gifting the business to one child as opposed to all of your children has the potential of causing jealousy and strife among the lot of them. Unfortunately, if you want to see your business continue to succeed, granting its control to *one* familial successor may be absolutely unavoidable. As previously mentioned, the same influences that caused your children to fight over childhood toys are the same influences that will cause them to tear your business apart.

Take our example of the Marlowe family that was introduced above. If the final scenario were to play out (i.e. all three children had passed their five-year audition with flying colors and all three of them demonstrated equal interest in assuming leadership and ownership in the company) whom would Darren Sr. choose? *How* would he choose? What about splitting control equally between the three? Would they be able to share things peacefully?

The next cause for conflict comes from the extended family (and all their well-intentioned – and sometimes boisterous – advice). In-laws have a way of adding a damaging perspective to any conflict that otherwise would have been completely alien to the family morale. This is especially true when it comes to determining the rightful successor. This is because in-laws haven't been around as long as everyone else. They simply don't understand the historical and familial significance of the family business. They cannot empathize with the degree of pride associated with its success – they'll only see its monetary value and what it can do for the lifestyle of their own satellite family.

Returning to the Marlowe family, let's add another ingredient into the mix. What if Darren Sr.'s nephew Ty had also demonstrated an excellent track record with the company? What if he'd been around longer than any of Darren Sr's children and had proven himself an integral part of the company's success? What if Ty's mother or father were completely contentious and alarmingly outspoken?

Once the owner of a family business determines his/her successor(s), he/she is greeted by another sticky problem. There will inevitably be a difference of opinion among the would-be successors regarding the worth of the business. This derives from the role of each family member within (or without) the business itself. Those members of the family who are active within the business probably have a better understanding of its actual value. In other words, your successor, a family member who has served as a key company employee for many years, may agree that your business is worth 2.2 million dollars; an outside observer – your drama-queen sister-in-law – will most certainly believe that the business is worth 22 million. One way to circumvent this logistical inevitability is to have an accurate appraisal conducted by a third-party observer. More on this later.

The final – and perhaps most decisive – cause for conflict is derived from previously unresolved and completely unrelated conflict. It is often impossible for certain members of any family to remain objective and refrain from complicating the situation with other issues. Your mother-in-law still resents you for having to skip the annual Christmas party due to an emergency at work. She'll take it out on you when it comes time to pass the business to one of her grandchildren. Of course, she won't agree with your decision. As far as she's concerned, you're completely incompetent and untrustworthy – at least, until you atone for the Christmas party fiasco. Then, maybe, she'll manage to see the light. This is perhaps an overly dramatic portrayal of prior conflict, but let it be known that situations like these do have a tendency to tamper with your decision.

While there is no sure-fire method to avoiding family debate altogether, there are several ways to ease the pain of dealing with conflict. It is important, first of all, for you to remember the wise words: Fair does not always mean equal and equal does not always mean fair. More importantly, you must make your family understand as well.

Fair is not always equal: One way to pass your business on to one child and still ensure that you have treated all of your children fairly is by gifting all of the non-successor children with a relative sum of cash or property. This can be a sticky issue, however, because most owners of family businesses are not, in fact, wealthy enough to part with either cash or property before death. For some, maintaining a comfortable retirement requires that all assets (save the company) remain with their original holder. On top of that, even if the gifts are affordable to begin with, they must be paid for again by both donor and donee through the often crippling venue of gift taxation.

The answer to this dilemma is to make it clear to the as-yet-unrewarded children that their patience will be generously compensated within your will. The money and property that could not be parted with during retirement can be guaranteed upon death.

Even if there is no money or property to offer, non-successor children can be promised their due. Carefully structured life insurance policies can be an excellent way to ensure that all of your children are treated as fairly as possible. It is often the most effective vehicle for providing the necessary liquidity to balance the estate among heirs.

Equal is not always fair: Another important subject that we have yet to mention is that some of your heirs may have been active within the family business while some have not. How do you reward those who have helped build the business through a concentrated supply of what we like to call "sweat equity"? This is a twofold problem – and we will illustrate it, once again, with the cautionary use of fictional characters:

Harry has two sons; Robert and Jim. Harry owns a large, successful farm that lines the northern side of a small Midwestern town. Over forty years ago, when Harry began the family farm, it was just a small plot of land that seemed almost infertile. Robert has been working on the farm alongside his father for almost fifteen years. In that time, he has helped his father to turn the small plot of infertile land into one of the county's biggest agricultural operations.

During that time, Jim – just one year younger than his brother Harry – has cultivated a successful career in journalism. He has climbed the ladder from minimum-wage photographer to sharply-dressed upper executive. Though his career is important to him, as far as Jim's concerned, its value pales in comparison to the pride he has for the family farm.

Harry is quickly approaching retirement age. He simply cannot lead and maintain a steady and reliable regimen of daily chores any longer. He has decided that his two sons are close enough in age and respect to be able to run the family farm with pride and expertise and without considerable conflict. Control of the farm, he has decided, will be carved into two equal shares to be given to each of his sons. He is surprised, however, that when he makes the announcement to Robert and Jim, they are both visibly disappointed.

Why is this? Two reasons. Robert feels that his sweat equity over the last 15 years has entitled him to a greater share of the control. After all, without his contribution, the farm may not have reached its ultimate success. His disappointment derives from a feeling that he has been under-compensated. Surprisingly, Jim is disappointed for the same reason; under-compensation. He recognizes that his brother Robert has already received money from the farm over the course of the last 15 years. A $60,000 annual salary for a farmhand is a pretty sizeable income, after all. Jim feels that because he hasn't received this kind of money from the farm, he is now entitled to majority control.

So who is right? In a way, both are. Both Jim and Robert can make the claim that equal doesn't necessarily mean fair.

The only way to avoid this sort of conflict – and, believe us, this sort of conflict isn't exclusive to family farms – is to lay out your intentions in advance. In the opinion of the authors, active members of the family business have a role to play in its eventual success – and should be compensated accordingly. In other words, we tend to agree with Robert. Sweat equity is important and highly valuable. Should you also happen to agree, we have provided the table on the following page. It displays an effective formula for computing the value of sweat equity when it comes time to divide up your assets and retire.

Sweat Equity Table	
Years of Service	**Sweat Equity**
1	1%
3	3%
5	6%
7	10%
10	15%
12	19%
15	24%
20	32%

We provide the above table only as a sample or a guideline. You alone are capable of crafting the sweat equity table that makes the most sense for your business.

Still, formulas and tables like this one are perhaps the only concrete ways to justify your decision to your heirs and family. Whether you back up your decision with charts and graphs or just plain old fashioned intuition, it is important that you open up the lines of communication well before the transition is announced. Without advanced warning, major life decisions like these can be startling and cause a great deal more anxiety than necessary – and this is exactly what conflict feeds upon. Make sure that your family knows the fate of your business before it comes time for that fate to make its turn. Telling all of your secrets has a way of making the family feel more involved – and by the time the decision is announced, you might avoid becoming the sole target for the dispute.

The Old Boss

So we have presented you with problems and we have presented you with potential solutions. When it comes down to it, no two businesses are alike – and, truly, there is no one better qualified to sum up what your business needs than you. You may not be the best person to evaluate your own children, but you do know full well what it will take for your family's business to continue to succeed.

So you now know the importance of assessing the potential, ability, and interest of your successor. You know that the family can be an obstacle and that businesses must sometimes be divided fairly and must sometimes be divided unfairly. You know that you must work towards a solution that leaves everyone feeling adequately compensated in the end. Even after you have all of the solutions to the problems outlined in this chapter etched in stone, you still have one question that remains to be answered – and it is perhaps the most difficult to assess and predict: Once your succession plan is laid out and the day arrives for you to retire, will you be able to let go?

A better question might be, "do you *have* to let go?" There are several levels of leadership that you may be able to maintain – such as staying on as a consultant or taking a permanent seat on an advisory board (something that may just put enough of yourself into the company to maintain a guiding interest without bogging you down so much). As long as you can remain objective enough to realize if and when your presence begins to damage the direction of the business, you may prove to be an invaluable asset to your successor. We will cover this topic in greater detail in chapter twelve.

Regardless of whether you plan to move into a cabin on a lake three states away or simply move out of the corner office and into one down the hall, you need to recognize that your time as sole leader has come to an end. While your opinions remain valid, they can no longer be considered sacrosanct. Relinquishing control (even if it is to someone you love) could very well be the most difficult thing for someone in your position to do.

There are several things to take to heart as you cope with the loss of something that has been your financial lifeblood (and indeed your driving force) for as long as your business certainly has. If you doubt the ability of your successor to carry on the proud tradition that is your family business, remember, Steve Jobs had a very different way of handling computers than Bill Gates. Sometimes you just have to step back and accept that the job will get done (and, in many cases, done well). Also, remember that you've done this before. Passing a business on to the next generation is much like the time when your son or daughter reaches his/her 18th birthday. Your advice will always be welcome – and, at times, may be very much needed – but, once the passage has been reached, the child (just as is the case with your company) must be allowed to stand on its own.

Chapter 7

Retaining Key Employees

Now that we have our successor in place, it's time to set him/her up with a dedicated workforce – those very same people who were so instrumental to your decades of success. It doesn't take a rocket scientist, but rather, simply a diligent reader who skimmed over the title of this chapter to recognize that we're talking about retaining key employees. It is no secret that a company cannot succeed without a well-trained and highly skilled staff (to say nothing of staff morale) so, obviously, the best way to manage a company in a transitional period is to insure that all employees remain focused and happy, right? Wrong.

A company is only as good as its worst employees. Take a minute to ponder that one.

But perhaps that is not the issue here. If you hadn't ironed out your employee problems by now, your company probably wouldn't have met with such success in the first place. The issue here is that many business owners mistakenly believe that it is their job to make sure all their employees stick around even if they, the owners, have no intention of sticking around themselves.

Perhaps the best practice for managing change is to retain as many of your key employees as possible – and the operative term here is "key". If we can assume this is true, it would be in your best interest to first identify your most important employees and then craft a logical plan on how to help these employees deal with such a significant change. For example, take Kathy in accounting. She basically runs the department by herself. She's worked for you for 20 years. You're all she's ever known when it comes to interacting with a boss. How is she going to handle the stress of answering to someone new after all these years? Or what about James from shipping? He's always looked up to you. It was his secret goal in life to rise to the top and work by your side, maybe even take the helm when you left. Will he respect the new leader?

In the case of a family business, the above scenarios can be taken one step further. What if Cousin Jerry, who runs your HR department, has always admired you, but thought very little of your daughter – your daughter who will be your successor? His distaste for her could stem from just about anything – and could be as insignificant as the time she cut in front of him in the buffet line during the family reunion dinner. In other words, when a business has multiple key employees from within the family, professional relations aren't the only issue – and, point of fact, when familial emotion is involved, may be the least of your concerns.

There are many questions you must ask yourself and situations you must contemplate. You must take an inventory (of sorts) of all your employees. Identify which ones your company cannot survive without and put a plan into action that keeps as many of them happy as is ethically and fiscally possible.

Change Management

The Tool Factor

Your first task to insuring that all of your employees remain happy and productive is perhaps the most difficult one. First and foremost, your employees look to their leader for guidance and support. Company morale is often dictated by the attitude and respectability of the uppermost manager. You must, therefore, be absolutely certain that the person you are training to take your place is not a tool (no pun intended). This is especially difficult for owners that intend to appoint a family member to take their place. We often view the capabilities of our relatives through rose-colored glasses.

The only way to remove these rose-colored glasses is by conducting a series of field tests. First of all, you should not be hiring somebody for your role who hasn't demonstrated success, or at the very least, potential for success, within your organization. Hiring someone from outside the organization, we suppose, is also acceptable provided this person has an excellent track record with companies at least remotely similar to your own. This being the case, it is relatively simple to see how apt your successor might be when it comes to employee retention. Appoint him/her to a leadership role within your organization while you are still the head honcho and allow several months/years for this person to prove capability. You will then be able to view the leadership potential of this person through the eyes of your employees. If the morale and productivity of your employees is clearly low, then you may consider another successor. If the morale and productivity of your employees is high, then you've found the right man/woman. If the attitude and output reflected by your employees isn't enough to help you make your decision, you may try directly asking them how they feel about your potential successor (though don't mention that he/she is your potential successor, of course).

Gardening for the Professional Realm

If you want to retain as many key employees as possible, you must take up gardening, specifically weeding, before your retirement begins. Just like you want to keep the prettiest flowers in your garden, in order to keep the best employees in your organization, you must weed out all of the non-key (so to speak) employees long before the leadership change takes place. If you're not particularly fond of botanical imagery, call it "removing the dead wood" (please only say that in your own mind, of course; not in front of the employees). The problem with dead wood is that it has a tendency to spread and infect the other, more useful wood. A poor employee is not only failing to meet his/her responsibilities, he/she may be greatly affecting the output and morale of your other employees. Nobody likes lugging dead weight. This is especially true during a transitional period. Any key employees left with the charge of picking up the slack during the changeover may wind up seeking another job.

Rewards Reap Rewards

A simple rewards program may be the best way to maintain company morale and even shift focus away from an otherwise monumental change in company direction. There is nothing better for employee relations than offering stock options. It keeps the employee pool focused on improving business output and quality. This particular strategy has a dual purpose when considering a change in ownership, too. Companies that are owned in part by its employees are much more liquid – and far easier to sell or buy. It also leads to more stability during the transitional period since, in a sense, only a certain percentage of a company's leadership is stepping down.

Another interesting reward to consider is a bonus program. Before leaving – or perhaps even before announcing your departure – set down a list of goals for your employees that stretch far enough into the future to eclipse your own retirement. Keep that bonus on the horizon and your employees will continue to work for it long after you're gone.

A Collaborative Effort

The final strategy is perhaps the most intriguing. The best way to take the focus off the stress of losing an old leader and gaining a new leader is to grant more leadership to your key employees. This does not necessarily mean promoting every important player in your business either. Consider building a broader culture of collaboration within your organization. Create and emphasize group projects. Applaud collaborative efforts. Pair up some of your biggest key players for your most important tasks. If your key employees have had a hand in every aspect of your company, then the shock of losing their boss (or another key employee, for that matter) is significantly minimized.

Coping with Change

There are those that suggest employee morale will never be lower than it is during a transitional period. Trust in the company will plummet, they say.

While these statements may be a little over-the-top, it is absolutely true that there will not be a single employee in your building that will be entirely stress-free during the transition (at least, the ones worth keeping won't be without stress). This stress often leads to a short-term decline in productivity, trust, and happiness. We all know that job-related stress can come from any number of different factors but, during a period of significant change, these factors, more or less, can be grouped into three major categories: Loss, Gain, and Family.

- Stress related to loss

This stress stems from the anxiety surrounding your departure. Other employees who leave or are being promoted to new jobs can also add to the pile. Basically, what loss-stress (if we can be so bold as to invent a term here) relates to is a difficulty coping with the loss of a daily routine or support structure. Any employee that loses a respected leader is likely to experience some form of stress related to that loss. Also, if an employee has grown accustomed to working alongside another employee and the latter employee has been promoted, demoted, fired, or quit, loss-stress is likely to come bubbling to the surface.

- Stress related to gain

During the succession planning process, you are likely to consider a wide range of people to promote into roles of greater responsibility (your successor being an obvious example). There may also be people that need to be shifted into roles of equal, but differing responsibility. In either case, these people are likely to experience a great deal of gain-stress (if we can invent yet another hyphenated term here) in the short-term. A new position brings new tasks and responsibilities and perhaps different co-workers. How will your employees handle being promoted? Will they honestly and confidently believe that they can perform all the tasks necessary to their new job?

- Stress related to family

It is no secret that familial relationships can be incredibly stressful. Throw working relationships on top of the familial ones, add a pinch of either loss- or gain-stress, and you've got one whopper of a situation to cope with. Just as with most businesses, families are set up in a hierarchical form. Any time this hierarchy is upset or subverted by the professional hierarchy, stress is likely to be induced. If your cousin Jerry that we mentioned earlier has clear memories of teaching your daughter how to ride a bike, how is he going to react to the prospect of taking orders from her at work?

Stress is inherent to any period of change. There is no way around it. Fortunately, you can curtail the adverse effects that stress may inflict upon your company with proper planning for the transition and plenty of communication with your family and employees every step of the way.

Identifying Employee Responses to Change

No preventative effort would be complete without a strong focus on pre-assessment. Obviously, it is impossible to predict to any certain degree which of your employees will stay and which will leave. It is true, after all, that people often speculate that their actions in tumultuous situations will be far more stable than they actually wind up being. Asking yourself a series of questions that zone in on each employee's potential actions is essential to proper succession planning.

First off, you must ask yourself, "Who in my company will be hurt the most emotionally by my departure?" Is there someone in your office that has grown attached to you on a personal level? Is there anyone that respects and admires you so greatly that they may not be able to imagine following the guidance of anyone else? Is there anyone that you might be passing over as your successor that would be personally offended when you make the announcement? Are any of these people members of your family? With the exception of the last question (unless your life mirrors that of a daytime soap opera), these, obviously, can be very difficult questions to answer objectively. Seeking a third party, such as a trusted advisor or family member within your organization, may be the key to determining just exactly who might be your most emotionally invested employees.

Next, you must decide who, if anyone, has something to lose professionally. Is there anyone that might feel threatened by the prospect of a new boss? Is there anyone that might feel like they were on the "fast track" to taking over your position and will only wind up being let down once the announcement is made? Are there others that might be promoted as a part of the process? And, if so, will they be able to handle the new responsibility?

The above two paragraphs outline questions relating to the biggest investments any employee makes in his/her company. Obviously, these investments can be either personal or professional – and directly dictate things such as work ethic, productivity, job satisfaction, and leadership ability. If you can comfortably and confidently seek out the answers to all of the above questions, you may be able to secure many of your key employees for the future of your organization.

We're not done throwing questions at you though. Now that we've tackled the issue of pre-assessment, we can move on to the issue of clear communication. While walking the unsteady line of succession planning, you may take to heart one certainty: if you don't clearly communicate to your employees (and family) on the subjects of why you are leaving and why your company will be just fine after you leave, your successor will have a difficult time trying to keep them happy both during and after the transition.

Now for the questions:

- Does everybody truly understand why I'm leaving?
- Did the announcement come as a shock?
- Has anybody demonstrated any objections to my leaving?
- Have I clearly communicated that my employees' job security remains intact?
- Does everybody know what they have to gain by my leaving?

These questions are important to reflect upon once you've made the announcement because the typical human reaction to change, especially dramatic and sudden change, is often all fire and brimstone. Be sure to assuage any anxiety that may surround your departure and your successor will have a much easier time maintaining a happy, secure, and stable employee base.

La Résistance

Of course, it would be overly simplistic to suggest that an attempt to calm things down would be sufficient to retain all your key employees. Think of your departure as a (hopefully) slightly less bloody political coup. Just as with any revolution, or major family decision, for that matter, you will have both supporters and detractors.

Theoretically, if you make the announcement of your departure and your eventual successor known to both the company and your family long before you leave, la Résistance will be a much less significant effort. Applying and addressing the questions listed in the previous segment will also be to your advantage. Unfortunately, there is no method that can guarantee a completely content employee base.

There are several schools of thought when it comes to dealing with the more resistant of your employees. Many would suggest that you simply hand them their walking papers. It's far easier to deal with a problem if it isn't working two doors down from your office, after all. The trouble with this method is that laying off your most vocal workers (which would definitely sum up the personalities of most parties involved in any resistance effort) tends to have adverse effects on company morale. Also, some of your most vocal members are likely to be members of your family as well – and you can't exactly evict them from the family in conjunction with your decision to evict them from their office. Getting rid of workers that clearly aren't pulling their weight is one thing. Getting rid of workers or family members that clearly (and perhaps compellingly) aren't happy with your decision to retire is entirely another.

Due to this negative impact, we suggest a method completely at odds with the norm – one that Presidents Lincoln and Truman employed very successfully within their cabinets. It is rarely effective in the long term to fight fire with fire. Showing your most contentious employees the door often leads to your most valuable employees finding the door all on their own. Rather than handing down harsh sentencing to your biggest detractors, why not try offering them roles of greater responsibility? There is nothing more flattering than being asked for help. Put la Résistance in charge of your most important transition-related tasks and they are far less likely to object. Helping out with a transitional period, after all, tends to give one the impression that one is shaping the company's future. Ask for their recommendations on people to promote or, where applicable, offer them promotions directly. Ask them for their opinions on how to improve company morale during the transition. Ask them for their advice on how to make your successor's first weeks/months go as smoothly as possible.

Don't fire your detractors. Ask for their advice. You may be amazed at how quickly such flattery and responsibility can calm la Résistance.

The Right Person in the Right Job

How your staff gets along with the top brass and each other while you are at the helm will undoubtedly change when management shifts and a new leader takes the reins. Maybe it was your style to crack jokes and bring in doughnuts every Friday. Perhaps your successor is more serious and lacks your infectious sense of humor, yet remains the most capable leader and most qualified to be the new boss. Every personality is different and how personalities mesh or don't mesh is an area to be dealt with even if you aren't considering passing the torch for a few more years. Any business would be wise to analyze how their people tick.

Each member of your staff and your family is an individual with unique strengths and weaknesses. It would behoove you to recognize those characteristics and their personality traits to make sure your successor and your current key employees are in the right roles. Just because your son has always been in sales doesn't mean that is the best position for his skills. Fitting folks into the right spot is best for them and for your business. It's well worth the small investment of time and money.

As we discussed in the previous chapter, you need to *ask* your successor if he/she even wants your job and you need to ask your key employees if they feel they are in the right position to best serve their goals as well as those of the company. Very often, in family businesses especially, people find themselves in a career role that isn't right for them. Joe is in accounting because that's where the job opening was when he graduated college. Maybe Joe even has an accounting degree and is a brilliant accountant. But maybe Joe just really hates math, too.

Crunching numbers comes easy, but he'd much prefer dealing with people and creating change in the product line. He has vision and ideas and is frustrated to be stuck behind a desk all day manipulating spreadsheets.

It happens all the time. We follow a career path laid out before us because that is what is expected, even more so when a family business is involved. Many people are in a particular career due to family expectations. How many times have you heard that Martin is a lawyer because his father was a lawyer and his grandfather was a lawyer? Martin grew up knowing he'd be a lawyer and never fought the issue. Maybe he thought he wanted to be a lawyer. Only, once he became one, he realized he'd rather be a stuntman or something.

Square pegs are forced into round holes time and time again. It doesn't have to be this way. You can assess the talent, interest and personality of your family and staff and have them switch roles. This way, more of the positions within your company tend to suit the individual. The process is not as hard as it may seem and does not require any magic.

Assessment tools such as aptitude tests and personality profiles may actually be appreciated by your crew. This is simply because many folks labor for years, never speaking up about how unhappy they are in their job. Give them a chance to speak out (however anonymously) and witness their eagerness to do so. Plus, imagine the boost in productivity that comes with happy workers in jobs that are a match for their skills and personalities.

One such assessment tool that we advocate is called DiSC® which is an acronym for four basic behavioral tendencies: dominance, influence, steadiness, and conscientiousness. Without even knowing more than that, can you place yourself into one of those categories?

People with a high *dominance* behavioral tendency seek to shape their environment by overcoming opposition to accomplish results. That may be you, the risk taker, the mover and shaker. Being a business owner means that you are up for a challenge and that you get things done. However, it can also mean that you lack patience for people who don't share your vision. Not everyone can be the most dynamic person in the room. The world, and your company, needs the big idea guy *and* the follow-through team. Always remember your business is a team effort. Helping the team to get along and function well together is important too. But we get ahead of ourselves. That's what someone in the steadiness camp would tell you.

Someone with a strong *influence* factor works their world by influencing and persuading others. They can say, "Hey kids let's put on a show," and you find yourself saying, "Okay!" You may have invented the greatest widget known to mankind, but if you don't have the influence, your widget will never sell. Many a widget lays unknown because the dominance guy thought he could make it alone.

No successful enterprise, not even that of Donald Trump, can make it as a one-man operation. The person with the *steadiness* behavioral tendency seeks to cooperate with others in order to carry out his/her tasks. Teamwork and the desire for harmony (and maybe the Christmas potluck luncheon) are hallmark characteristics of this person.

The worker with a strong *conscientiousness* tendency works within existing circumstances to ensure quality and accuracy. Somebody has to keep track of the widgets and the profits, after all. Popularity is not a priority for this type of person, but order in the office most certainly is. Details matter and somebody in the outfit has to keep the train on the track.

Every one of us incorporates all four of these tendencies in our personality – only they are incorporated in differing intensities. This is good: every business needs all four tendencies if it hopes to survive. This is also bad: differing personalities don't always get along.

The dominance person may be swirling a hundred miles an hour with ideas and energy, but gets easily irritated when the conscientiousness person says, "That's not in the budget." The dominance guy is a force – and every successful business needs that force – but every business also needs the nuts and bolts attention-to-detail person who makes sure the bills, taxes, and workers get paid. The dominance and the conscientiousness look out at the world from their own very separate and distinct points of perspective. For them, trying to be in the other guy's shoes is literally like attempting to live on another planet.

Now imagine that these two personality types are brothers who are taking over shared leadership once dad has retired. Difference in opinion is guaranteed to happen. How they handle the inevitable conflicts will depend on whether you, the very wise owner, has embarked upon the personality profile with your core of key players. Having family and staff take a formal assessment will alert them to their own traits and also to those of the people they work with. When working closely together in a family business, it helps to understand each other. Brothers Jack and John are total opposites, but if they can come to terms with each other's limitations and realize each is hard-wired that way, it will be easier to steer the ship along a mutually agreeable course.

We are who we are and we need to work with who we are. No, that's not a Dr. Seuss line, it's just another way to explain that people's personality traits are just as important as their intelligence; their overall ability and effectiveness in their job depends upon a proper match of skills and personal style.

Believe it or not, we are not a paid commercial endorsement for the DiSC® personal assessment program. We just feel that – if for no other reason than it is the original, oldest, and most widely accepted form of personal assessment on the market – it is the best available tool to assess the skills, tendencies, and desires of your employees. We tend to think of ourselves as originals, too, after all.

Having the right person in the right position seems so obvious, but time and time again, companies fail to live up to the task. Fortunately, the problem is easily rectified. Whatever assessment tool you choose, at least choose one. You will be enlightened, your employees and family members will feel empowered, and your company will reap the benefits.

~~~

As you've known all along, your business success is attributed to the great team that you have managed to assemble over the years. Their experience, ability, and dedication have helped build your company into what it is today. It is impossible to put a price tag on employee relations, but having a well-oiled, smooth running staff is yet another asset to add to the appeal for your buyer.

And now that we mention it, have you, by this point, been wondering what your business is really worth? If not, why not? Answers lie on the following page.

Section 4:
Preparing for and Completing the Sale

Chapter 8

What's Your Business Really Worth (And Why Should You Care)?

– The first day I think about selling my business is the first day I start it.

The above quip may seem rather cryptic. It could mean so many different things to so many different people. The heart of the matter is, however, that selling a business is extremely complicated. This is exactly why an entire chapter on business appraisals is warranted.

With this chapter, we reveal the notable points associated with the task of having a business appraised. After highlighting the several reasons why you should care about the value of your business, we will elaborate on the steps to take when selling to a buyer either inside or outside of the family. It is a common misconception that one should value a business differently (read "low-ball it") if selling to a loved one than if selling to a total stranger. This isn't always the case. An accurate and complete valuation of the business is always advantageous (even if it tends to price things out of the anticipated range). More on this topic in chapter 9.

Topics covered in this chapter include when and how often to get an appraisal, reasons for doing so, what it will cost, who to trust in order to ensure that it's accurate, seven different ways to evaluate your business, and an important concept that will be known henceforth as "the Two Values."

This chapter is headed by two questions – and it can be supposed that the latter question is actually the most critical to address. And why *should* you care? Allow us to explain:

Why You Should Care

The D's (Again)

We hate to sound like a warped record but, once again, we have to remind you of the dangerous D's.

We've already beaten to death the concept that a buy/sell agreement is absolutely essential in order to circumvent any and all of the dangerous D's, but we have not yet addressed its relationship to a proper business appraisal. Here it is, laid on thick: While a buy/sell agreement is paramount to any business that wishes to embark upon succession with ease, without a proper and accurate business appraisal, it may not be worth the paper it's printed on.

And here's why: So you've endured a hardship – maybe a death in the family or a particularly squalid divorce – and, due to your well-planned and well-implemented buy/sell agreement, your business has passed through without missing a step; but has the buyer paid enough for the business? If you're the buyer, we suppose that this issue is fairly irrelevant if not pleasantly avoidable, but if you're the seller – or someday intend to be the seller – perhaps you should read on.

The Two Values

In order to fully address the reasons why you should care about business appraisal, we must now flesh out the concept of the Two Values. The Two Values refer to: 1) What's the business worth to me and my family? and 2) What's the business worth to the buyer?

The first Value is fairly simple to address. Most likely, in yours and your family's opinion, the business is worth far more than the fair market value may suggest. Why is this? Simply put: Because you've spent years of hard labor and financial risk to bring this business to its feet. You've toiled and triumphed – and there is a great deal of priceless sentiment attached to such an accomplishment. The business, in essence, becomes a part of the family.

The business, furthermore, may end up *defining* the family. Successful businesses have a tendency to project outward into the community. Through years of economic development and community giving, your business may have developed its own unique identity – one that is securely attached to you and your family. Few businesses illustrate this concept quite so effectively; but think of the Rockefellers. Across decades, this particular family business was so successful and so charitable that people tend to equate the family name with honor, charity, and prestige (to say nothing of an almost obscene amount of wealth). Not every business has a national presence – but the same kind of essence exists in every community, however small. Your business, within your town, state, or region, may represent a microcosm of the Rockefeller effect.

So, considering these influences – sweat equity and family pride – what kind of price is demanded by the typical family business owner? We, the authors, can assure you that, more often than not, the number is absolutely staggering.

The second of our Two Values is flagrantly different. Also, allow us to reiterate that all of these concepts can be applied to either the scenario of an outside buyer or the scenario of a buyer within the family, but it is not our intention to specifically focus on one scenario or the other. Whatever the case, we'll illustrate the concept of the second Value by creating a fictional buyer – and because we are wildly inventive authors, we'll call him John Smith.

John Smith is in position to purchase a new business but, like any intelligent buyer with an intelligent advisor, he's not looking to just roll up to the local convenience store and buy a new job. Ownership is hard work and he knows it. Without the promise of a healthy payout, he's probably not going to pull out his wallet and take the risk.

So what's the first thing that Johnny looks for? Profits. More specifically: *excess* profits. We have to remember that John, whether he's your son, great nephew, or a complete stranger, may not have the same kind of investment or pride in your family business that you do. Without the potential to begin making money on his investment immediately, John may not have much desire to embark upon this new venture. John's the kind of guy who would rather give up his independence than his money stack. In other words, he'd sooner work for someone else than break his back running his own, unprofitable business.

Following along these same lines, John doesn't even care to consider a price tag that will require him to make payments for more than five years. He wants to make money. Having to dish to the bank all of his profits over the next decade is less than desirable as far as John's concerned. If a large and long-term financial investment is required to own your business, John will surely take a pass on your asking price.

In addition to this bias, John is terribly concerned with the fair market value of the business and what the business owns. Your decades-old tractor may carry a great deal of sentimental value to you, but all John sees is a rusty and outdated piece of equipment. Without excess profit, your business is only worth what it can show in labor, product, and equipment and, without valuable labor, product, and equipment, your business, to John, may very well seem worthless.

The bottom line is that, according to the trend of the second Value, John will only be concerned with what the appraiser has to say about the worth of your business. Without an accurate and unbiased appraisal, you may find it very difficult to attract the attention of buyers like John – even if John happens to be your son.

Tracking Your Progress

The final – and rather simple – reason that you should care about what your business is worth is that it is an excellent way to track your progress. Oftentimes, when confronted with the prospect of relying on an outside source to appraise a business, most owners get defensive and fail to see the importance of such an action. This is what we like to call the "who could possibly know my business and what it's worth better than I do?" syndrome. Don't let it creep up on you. The answer to this question is that – hands down – a qualified business appraiser knows more about the value of your business than you do. No question.

And why is this? He/she is unbiased. He/she employs one of several time-tested theorems to ensure the accuracy of the appraisal. He/she has nothing to gain by tweaking the numbers.

We digress. The point of this segment is that a regular business appraisal can actually help a company's direction and prospects. The reason is simple: It's much more difficult to know where you're going if you don't know where you stand. Without a regular affirmation of your business' value, how can you possibly know what level at which you are operating and, therefore, what kind of success you are capable of achieving? Rest assured, this kind of directional certainty is difficult to come by on your own.

Even when presented with the above argument, most owners still feel that outsourcing a business appraisal is an unnecessary and unwanted expense. If you are one of these people, consider this: A quality appraisal always incorporates myriad different valuations and applies only those most appropriate to your business. This means that, just by trying to figure out the exact value of your business, you could discover how much your competitors' businesses are selling for. You will also learn key points like the numbers associated with your product lines, division/line growth or slow down, inventory turnover, the average date of receivables, average liability pay, return on equity, and many others. A simple appraisal, therefore, can be a highly effective way for you to discover the strengths and weaknesses within your organization, pin-pointing exactly which departments and disciplines are succeeding and which should provide most cause for concern. With this information, you could more effectively pass judgments on your company and enjoy a greater and more disciplined sense of success. Your earnings and output will improve and the expense associated with hiring a business appraiser will be repaid tenfold.

When Should I Get an Appraisal? How Often Should I Get an Appraisal? What Does It Cost?

Whoa, slow down there. That's a lot of questions. The answer to the first question is simple: If you've never had an appraisal, get one done immediately. For all of the reasons listed above, you won't regret it. If you have had an appraisal done before, getting it updated is both quick and comparatively inexpensive.

In answer to the second question, our humble recommendation is that you have your business appraised regularly (optimally, you should space them out in intervals of 2 years or less). In addition, if you ever run into a significant change in the company, such as a change in the leadership structure or the cutting/adding of a product line, you should re-evaluate immediately.

And to the money question, it's complicated. Each appraisal, obviously, is run on a business-by-business basis. It is a service like any other – and the price tag fluctuates based on the qualifications and experience of the appraiser and the size and complexity of your company. It is a necessary business expense, so bite the bullet and get it done.

Who Do I Turn To if I Want to Sell to an Outside Party?

The Banker Principle

Most often, owners of family businesses do not even consider ordering an appraisal until their bankers prompt them to do so. Unfortunately, in these circumstances, some bankers do not also advise their clients that a certified business appraiser would be the most qualified professional for the job. This is perhaps because it is not in the best interests of the banks to ensure that you get a fair – and full – price for your family business.

This may seem odd, but remember, a banker's job is to protect his/her interests and his/her bank's assets. As a result, his/her most driving influence tends to be to set the appraisal at a level that is comfortable for his/her bank to lend.

Should the business falter or even go bankrupt, the bank is forced to take one of two actions: either they fold and accept the sizeable monetary loss or they attempt to run the business themselves. Neither route is terribly appealing. Thus, your banker is likely to set the price of your business right around its "fire-sale" value.

In summary, due to a variety of influences, appraisals carried out by bankers are often quite low.

The Accountant Principle

Some might think that the answer, then, is to seek the counsel of an accountant. After all, who could possibly know the numbers associated with your business better than he/she? Probably no one.

It is true that your accountant could and would closely and accurately appraise your business. However, it is not advisable to hire an in-house accountant for the job. This is because his/her opinion may end up carrying very little weight if the appraisal value is ever challenged. Most prospective buyers or banking lenders will not put credence into an appraisal created by someone on your payroll.

Evaluations really should be left to a competent third party appraiser. This appraiser has nothing to gain by over- or under-pricing the business in question and could therefore be trusted by all parties involved. Even if the sale price winds up being contested in court, a third party appraiser will be more comfortable defending his/her decision.

As one of the authors of this book also happens to be a business broker, we can say without a shred of uncertainty or humility that any competent business broker would suggest that an outside appraisal conducted by a third party appraiser is the most appealing and trustworthy approach. And this isn't simply to ensure that the seller is getting the most out of the sale. It is fascinating how often the values presented by the owner and those presented by an appraiser will vary. Just as intriguing is the fact that just about the same number of owners tend to undervalue their companies as overvalue.

To illustrate, we offer a sample case, the details of which, for the sake of all parties involved, are intentionally vague. In our example, we have a business owner who was anticipating retirement and the sale of his business to his son. He indicated to the business brokers that he hoped to get $2 million for his business. The brokers, who were savvy enough to recognize industry averages, suggested that he seek an outside appraisal. Imagine the owner's surprise when the valuation was returned to him at over $14 million. Not only could he be sure to enjoy a comfortable lifestyle throughout his retirement, but he could rest a little easier knowing that his son had purchased a valuable business that was certainly on the fast track.

We would like to point out that this is certainly not the norm. However, it is not uncommon for the owner's opinion of value and the actual value of a particular family business to differ by ten to fifty percent.

The Answer

Since we've already alluded to it fairly regularly, the answer to the question of who you should turn to in order to evaluate your business should be abundantly clear by now. But, in the interest of chronology, we will award the notion with its own truncated summary segment.

The answer, if you don't already know, is that the only person you can fully trust to provide you with an accurate appraisal of your family business is a third party business appraiser. The other three professionals that most people turn to – their banker, accountant, or business broker – stand to gain too much by providing inaccurate and often unfair valuations. Furthermore, outside evaluations tend to speed up the negotiating process, prevent expensive and time-consuming litigation, and ensure that every party involved gets all that he/she can out of the successful sale.

The more credible your selected appraiser, the less likely he/she will be challenged by the buyer or financier. As we mentioned previously, it is rarely in your best interest to have the banker do the appraisal, so if the banker or a purchaser deem your third party appraiser to be credible, they may not feel the need to have an additional appraisal performed. Remember, appraisals are expensive for bankers, too.

Seven Different Ways to Evaluate Your Business

On the surface, it may seem rather arduous to employ seven different methods to evaluate your family business. Within these pages, however, you won't find the half of it. For the purposes of discussion, we will concentrate our efforts on the different – and important, effective, etc. – evaluation methods for private companies only. Public companies incorporate another level of value interpretation that would expand this book into volumes.

Theoretically, the values of businesses are relatively simple to calculate: numerical data plugged into given formulas. It's like 10th grade math – punching numbers into a calculator and scrawling them down on the page. If you hated 10th grade math, we apologize, and, in truth, we sympathize (we hated it too).

What's important in valuing a business is relative variance – hence the need to outline seven distinct methods. The variances lend to the emotional influences of the buyers, sellers, or lenders. Quantifying and formalizing the emotional subjective tendencies tends to quell any arguments or nervous ticks. The more formulas utilized, the more rigid the conclusions and the less chance for subjected emotion.

And now, the fun stuff. The Internal Revenue Service (Revenue Ruling 59-60) – as well as most of the established appraising societies – requires the appraiser to use all approaches for which there is reliable and pertinent data. Section 3 of this ruling – under Approach to Valuation – recognizes that appraising is not an exact science. The statement reads, true to IRS form, rather dryly, "A sound valuation will be based upon all the relevant facts, but the element of common sense, informed judgment and reasonableness must enter into the process of weighing those facts and determining their aggregate significance."

So, that being said, we'll move on to a short discussion of each of our seven methods – following a light disclaimer: Let it be known that every appraiser has his/her own set of evaluation methods and his/her interpretation of their relevance (this isn't, in fact, the end-all, be-all of business appraisals). All we offer is the methods that are most commonly employed and some samples.

Asset Value Method

The Asset Value Method represents the estimated value of all tangible and intangible assets. This formula begins with a fair market value (FMV) assessment of assets. Then, an industry common multiplier is attached. This value is generally added to the year's net cash flow in order to determine a market value.

It looks a little something like this:

ASSET METHOD

Equipment and Equity	$11,249
Improvements	$0
Vehicles	$0
Stock/Supplies	$0
Licenses/Patents	$0
Asset High	$12,374
Asset Low	$10,124

Capitalization Method (Cap Rate Method)

A capitalization method (Cap Rate) incorporates discretionary cash flow divided by a rate of return associated with the level of risk. This approaches the business from a pure investment perspective, revealing the yield it produces for the buyer or investor. When an investor assumes risk of any nature, it is assumed that, somewhere along the line, there will be reward for such risk. Essentially, the more risk endured, the better the potential of return on investment.

The Cap Rate can be concerned with several different elements: The time it takes for the investor to recapture the original investment; a multiple of earnings; or a percent rate of return. It can also demonstrate a return rate percentage at its highest peak and its lowest valley – along with a real dollar value that can be associated with those percentages. Observe (next page):

CAPITALIZATION

		Years		
1	2	3	4	5
		Cap Rates		
23%	22.4%	21.6%	21.9%	21.5%

High Return %	23%
Low Return %	21.5%
Capital Rate High	$330,543
Capital Rate Low	$308,986

Critical Factors Method

As the name might suggest, this method takes into account all of the "critical factors" that may persuade or dissuade a potential buyer from purchasing the company in question. These include:

- Percent of Down Payment
- Interest Rates, Type of Loan, and Term of Years
- Financing
- The Desirability of the Company
- Industry
- Contracts or Leases
- Types of Accounts
- The Economy

As mentioned earlier, emotions are quantified as best as possible in the evaluation process and many critical factors are buyer specific. Here is an example of the weighted percentages that might go into this most touchy and emotionally-charged method:

CRITICAL FACTOR

Financing	50%
Desirability	155%
Lease	77%
Economy	240%
Critical High	$386,910
Critical Low	$105,898

Debt Capacity Method

As a pure mathematical model, this calculation deducts cash expenses from direct business cash revenues and determines a "discretionary cash flow." Deductions are then made for the owner's salary, amortization, and depreciation of cost of assets. The result is discretionary cash for debt service.

This analysis determines if the business can prosper with the debt service, given the level of discretionary cash. A sample follows (again…next page):

DEBT CAPACITY METHOD

Normalized Discretionary Earnings	$120,317
Less: Management Compensation	$47,000
Less: Economic Depreciation	$2,250
Adjusted Normalized Earnings	$71,067
Interest Rate	7.00%
Fast Payout Years	5
Slow Payout Years	8
Debt High	$434,382
Debt Low	$299,085

Comparable Sales Method

This method utilizes the actual sales of like or similar companies found within an industry. The calculations are usually the result of a selling price ratio. Of course, the sale price, location, product(s), revenues, etc., are all researched to better define the comparables used. Here is an example (you guessed it…next page):

COMPARABLE SALES METHOD

Target	$188,916
Labor	88%
Predictability	184%
Management	84%
Competition	53%
Revenue	100%
Longevity	111%
Location	50%
Loanability	50%
Clientele	33%
Liability	75%
Weighted High	$156,686
Weighted Low	$67,339

Industry Factor Method

This method bears a number of weighting factors applicable to the critical factors mentioned previously. The "weighting" is an attempt to recognize the change or shift in economic conditions relevant to the industry in question. As the motivating factors of critical risks are tabulated mathematically, these functions seem to simulate how emotions relate to current and future conditions. A detailed illustration (Yep):

INDUSTRY RISK FACTOR

Base Value	$366,583
Competition	$131,970
Management Type	($10,997)
Turnover	$76,982
Type of Business	$62,319
Owner Finance Years	$36,658
Owner Finance Rate	$241,945
Owner Finance %	$43,990
Bank Finance Years	$36,658
Bank Finance Rate	$91,646
Bank Finance %	$0
Number of Employees	$62,319
Age of Industry	$98,977
Industry Market	$87,980
Years of Operation	$168,628
Consulting Time	$58,653
Net Cash – Salary	$62,319
Local Economy	$98,977
Labor Market	$40,324
Skills Required	($32,992)
Union Strength	($157,631)
Location	$472,892
National Economy	$43,990
National High	$90,356
National Low	$88,106

Multiple or Average Value Method

This method is a composite or summation of all of the previously mentioned valuation methods with the purpose of determining an average price a "reasonable" person in "reasonable" times would pay for a company.

Generally, appraisers will set values within ranges to establish a maximum and minimum level based on data and estimates.

And Now a Quiz

We're kidding, of course. There will be no quizzes here. That is why you hire the professionals who can crank out those variations in their sleep. We can, however, recommend a cure for insomnia: reading some Revenue Rulings.

So as you prepare for the sale of your business, you now have come to a very astute revelation. If, in the course of your operations, you needed a welder and that was not your trade, you didn't do it yourself, you hired a welder. If you needed a new roof put on your building, you called a roofer. Apply that same principle now. You are not a business appraiser. Although you know how to run your business better than anyone else, when it comes to determining what your business is worth in today's market, you need to make a call. But who should you call? The banker, the business broker, the accountant? No. The butcher, the baker, the candlestick maker? No. You should call an independent third-party business appraiser. This simple act will prevent you from under- or over-valuing your business and, subsequently, you won't lay awake at night second-guessing the sales price. We want you to have a good night's sleep tonight and every night of your upcoming, well-earned retirement.

Selling your business is difficult on many levels. We understand and respect that. Once you have made the determination that now is the right time for you to step down and pursue other wants, wishes, and whims, it is time to figure out how to make your business worth as much as possible. Or, rather, it is time to enhance the value of your company for the new buyer.

Chapter 9

Enhancing Value for the New Buyer

Now that we've browbeaten you into accepting the importance of a business appraisal, we must now move on to the finer points of selling.

Establish What Might Make Your Business Seem Appealing

Clunky though this section header may be, what it calls for is absolutely essential. Before you even consider selling anything, you must first evaluate whether or not it's worth buying. Otherwise, you'll be left in the cold, the sale item remaining forever up for bids.

The same concept applies when selling your family business to a successor. Remember, if the successor is a family member, by establishing what makes your business most appealing, you'll be helping yourself out twice. First of all, you will be able to determine all of the areas where your business is good and all of the areas where it could use some improvement. Secondly, you will be categorizing all of the attractive features that your business boasts – leveraging your best qualities for the sale.

Regarding this topic, some points of interest we feel obligated to cover include clientele, location, and service.

Beginning with clientele, it is easy to see that businesses with larger numbers of clients are far more attractive than businesses with just a few. This is because it is much easier for the new buyer to earn back his/her investment if there is already a broad and reasonably stable pool of clients in place. Without this, your successor may end up having to spend hundreds of thousands, if not millions, of dollars to bring in new clients. So remember this equation: More clients = More value. We'll discuss this concept later in greater detail – within the curiously titled segment, *The Whale Factor*.

Following along our line of thought, location is the next most important point to cover. Most people understand the significance of location. If you don't, then you're probably not a terribly successful business owner, and would therefore have little use for this book, so we won't spend too much time on this subject. It must be stated, however, that the same quality location that allowed your business to boom is the same quality location that will allow your business to sell for a much larger sum. If your successor is a family member, you can rest assured that it will aid him/her in achieving the goal of continued success well into the future.

Of our three listed points of interest, the final is perhaps the most widely misused. When you first read the header of this chapter, the first area of appeal that jumped into your head was "service," wasn't it? It's okay. For some reason, everybody thinks of service first. But let it also be known that *everybody* thinks – or, rather, assumes – that their business boasts superior quality service. That's just the nature of the beast. The dicey bit about service is that there aren't many accurate measures of service that an owner can employ. So how do you know if your service is as excellent as you think it is? We will discuss a few tried-and-true methods later in the segment entitled *Covert Ops*.

The bottom line is while all of these areas of interest are effective measures of your business and its value, and all of them can be dressed up and improved in order to enhance value for the new buyer, it is unlikely that you, the owner, are capable of appraising them to the fullest potential. It is *always* better to have an outside consultant come in and weigh things for you. He/she will not hesitate to tell you exactly where you need to improve.

Use Common Sense

Clean It Up

We begin with the obvious. The simple act of cleaning things up greatly increases the appeal of your company.

If you've ever sold a home, you understand the work to be done to best portray the home's quality and charm. Vacuum, sweep, mop, and scrub. Oftentimes, special services must be ordered such as woodwork touch-ups or carpet stretching. All of this to ensure that the potential buyer is exposed to the best possible face your home has to offer.

The same is true for a business. Perception is reality and appearance is everything. Offices must seem efficient and well-kept; warehouses must be streamlined and uncluttered; equipment must be functional and up-to-date. Before the potential buyer is given the tour of your property, you must take action to dress things up accordingly. An untidy and inefficient workplace is an unattractive one. Many business owners mistakenly believe that a factory is expected to be grungy and have grease on the floor. Maybe so, however, to the prospective buyer a clean shop versus a filthy factory makes an impression. It is a reflection of your overall business and, right or wrong, can give an indication to them how you take care of your business. Like your mama told you, appearance matters. And your handwriting teacher in second grade was right, neatness counts. Be sure to spend whatever necessary in order to improve the physical appeal of your business and your money will be paid back in spades.

The Whale Factor

As we have already mentioned, businesses with large numbers of clients are far more appealing to the buyer than businesses with smaller numbers. We have not yet mentioned that small numbers of clients are sometimes acceptable, given that the clients account for a large sum of residual money. A buyer who obtains a client pool of 1,000 that provides him with $100,000 in annual salary would probably be just as happy with a pool of 100 clients that provide him with the same. In fact, the buyer may actually prefer the smaller pool of clients because it would seem to require less work to produce the same income.

This is not true, however, if the business in question receives a large percentage of its earnings from one or two specific clients. If your business generates a great deal of money every year but 25% or more of that money comes from a single source – one whale of a client – then your business is far less appealing than a company with a more diversified client base. This is because a competent buyer will immediately recognize that, whenever a business changes hands, it stands to lose a few of its clients. If the buyer loses the whale, he/she's lost a great deal of revenue and probably stands to lose all of his/her money on the new business investment.

There is no easy solution to this predicament. On one hand, it is advisable for the seller to drop the whale client – or at least to focus more energy and attention on the other, lesser contributing clients – but this may cause the business to fail before it even reaches the selling point. On the other hand, it is advisable for the seller to keep the whale client, thereby maintaining the highest level of recordable revenue, but this action may make the business more difficult to sell, if not handicap the selling price altogether. Unfortunately, no two businesses are the same. What's right for one may not be right for another. So it is impossible for us to offer advice on this issue one way or the other.

Consult with a Consultant

The above predicament is exactly why there is such a high demand for consultants in today's financial world. Sometimes, even those owners with a great deal of common sense and business acumen require the wisdom of an outside source. Hiring a consultant to help you make key decisions such as what to do about a whale client or how to make your technologically-outdated production line seem adequately efficient is well worth the price.

Private vs. Public

The main distinction and truly the only thing that matters for our discussion is that the valuation, and thus the sales price, of a public company versus a privately held company will vary significantly. The distortion in valuations between the two is result of the volume of potential buyers (and sellers). Potential buyers of publicly traded companies can buy any fraction of the company their wisdom or pocketbook allows. Conversely, the sale of a private company means the purchase of the entire entity and that shrinks the pool of buyers. Long ago and in a galaxy far away, most family owned businesses were small operations, privately owned, and the notion of going public was rarely entertained. That is not the case today. Family businesses can be public or private. And now as you approach the time to sell, a viable place to sell your family owned business could very well be to a public company. We know a local pharmacist who built an independent drug store with a nice pharmacy clientele and was very pleased to sell his single-owner operation to a publicly-held national drug store chain.

The difference between public and private is dollars. When talking valuation, public companies use a myriad of methods but most will at least consider the price-earnings ratio, which is the current stock price of a company divided by the earning per share, the result tells how much investors are willing to pay per dollar of earnings. A price-earnings ratio of 20 suggests that investors are willing to pay $20 for every $1 of net earnings that the company generates. A private company of course has a much lower value in the financial realm and commonly gets two to five times its earnings. These valuations reflect in the potential for lending, as well. If a company is looking to expand and needs leverage, bankers will consider a much higher value and lend accordingly. They also understand that it's much easier to get their money back when they can immediately sell their shares versus trying to sell an entire company in a generally difficult situation. So, back to our discussion…if an owner is considering public versus private on company value only, it will be hard to ignore the potential of going public. Obviously, we did not discuss all of the issues in the consideration of going public simply because you would not be able to carry this book home.

Tricks of the Trade

Covert Ops

That's right, the world of espionage is not exclusive to the geopolitical stage. It plays a large part in enhancing the value of your own company too. It should be noted that, while the tactics outlined in this segment are excellent for enhancing value for the new buyer, they are also very effective for those business owners who simply wish to get a leg up on the competition and help their companies advance to the next level.

The first stratagem to employ involves cleverly masking your identity – we recommend using a well-cloaked moniker such as "James Bond" – and masquerading as a potential customer/client interested in your competitors' products or services. This allows you to pass undetected through their system, listening over the phone lines as they reveal key intelligence such as their value proposition, quality of customer service, or marketing approach.

In all seriousness, treating yourself to a firsthand experience of your competitors' customer service is an excellent, easy, and often overlooked method to determining the strengths and weaknesses of all the key players within your market. Knowing these elements will help you better assess where you need to improve, how to position yourself against the competition, where to direct your value proposition, and, above all, how to enhance value for the new buyer.

There is one other covert operation to consider – although it carries the potential to be considerably more painful to you and your opinion of your organization and its staff. This one involves turning the tables on yourself. It's kind of like using a remote control device to access your business' true image within the mirror. This strategy calls for you to ask a friend – this friend must be as neutral as possible – to call your company and allow your employees to take him/her through all of the steps to becoming a new client.

The genius of this method is that it allows you to gain access and insight into the strengths and weaknesses of your own customer service staff. Not only that, but because it calls for using your trusted friend, you'd be likely to get the service for free. So, at little or no cost to you, you would receive the most accurate and untainted opinion of your organization possible. Again, knowing your company from the inside out will prove invaluable when it comes time to position your business for the sale.

Checking Your Excess Baggage

Everybody knows that the key to good business is to provide the customer with a wide range of products or services within an effectively synergized series of lines. When it comes to selling your business, however, this isn't always true.

Say you offer three different lines of products or services to the consumers within your market. They may be extremely complimentary towards one another – and it may make perfect sense that your family business provides all of them to your customers or clients – but if, before the sale, any one of those three different lines is failing, you would be doing yourself more harm than good to hold on to it.

A potential buyer is going to carefully study all aspects of his/her purchase. He/she will want to know exactly what he/she is getting for the proposed sum of money. As this is almost always the case, you can be certain that a faltering line of business will throw up a red flag in the potential buyer's mind. Unprofitable product or service lines are just like unprofitable businesses – they require a great deal of time, money, and effort to maintain and provide little, if anything, in return. As you can imagine, this particular type of red flag is less than desirable.

Some owners tend to believe that doing all that they can to massage the failing line of business back into success is the best way to go. During the time of a sale, however, it may not be advisable. This is because massaging a failing line of business takes a great deal more time and effort than you can or should be providing. Dressing a business up for sale takes focus and worrying about boosting the levels of a failing line of business presents a sizeable threat to that focus. All things considered, it would be in your best interest to simply discontinue the product or service in question.

Show Profit!

Selling the Company Car – and Other Obvious Notions

As we've alluded to, when attempting to sell your business, profit is everything. Without showing profit, your business may be doomed to stagnation. No well-informed buyer would take a risk on an unprofitable company. Get the money into the company now, show that profit, and you will reap profit at the time of the sale.

We do offer you a valuable nugget of truth: Don't structure your lifestyle and your business around the possibility of getting rich after the sale. In other words, don't run things in such a way that suggests you're looking forward to that pot of gold at the end of the rainbow. That pot of gold, after all, isn't always as quantifiable – or even as large – as your wildest dreams can provide. Make sure that you do everything you can to show profit and retain profit throughout your life. Build a nest egg. Don't rely on the sale. Think of the sale not as the cake but, rather, the icing, and you will find that a comfortable retirement is well within your reach. Remember, the object of a business is to sell it, but the other, more important object is to make money along the way, all the while enjoying the prospect of getting up and going to work every morning.

This brings us to the point highlighted by the segment's bold title: Show Profit! So you're not showing profit – what do you do? In addition to the obvious cutbacks that can be made within your own company's operations, we offer a few simple, no-brainer-style solutions. All of these solutions deal with cutting corners, saving money on everything that you can possibly manage to cut back on. The more cash you can squeeze out of the expense line of your business or lifestyle, the easier it becomes to show profit before the sale.

The reason that all these cutbacks are important is because any money shown in profit before the sale pays back dividends after the sale. The general rule is that every dollar shown in profit tends to pay back about 3½ dollars in revenue generated from the sale. So think of all of these recommended alterations to your workplace and lifestyle as temporary inconveniences. Once the sale is over, you can feel free to live 3½ times as "large."

Are you driving a $70,000 luxury car that is listed to your business? Well, come sale time, the party's over. When you're looking to trim the fat around the office, oftentimes the first and best place to look is in your parking space. Taking a cut in your own income by listing the car under your own name, or taking a cut in your lifestyle by selling the car altogether, will surely pay off when it comes time to sell your business. Every dollar counts and 70,000 of them is certainly a respectably high number.

Are you a travel junkie? There's nothing wrong with that, and in fact, we envy you. However, any money that could be dumped into showing profit for your company is money well spent. If you want the buyer to pay top dollar for your business, you may have to cut corners, if not cut entirely, on your travel expenses for at least one to two years before the sale. Remember, every dollar saved on travel generates 3½ for all future trips. Trade in your plane tickets to Orlando and look forward to buying tickets to Paris.

Are you overly generous to your family via your payroll? Now is the time to "get real." Your bottom line will improve greatly if you no longer pay your daughter a full-time salary while she is away at college. Ditto for your six-year-old son who is in first grade. Maybe your mother comes in everyday, but does nothing more than make a pot of coffee and do the crossword puzzle. Trimming the payroll will increase your profit and your salability.

This is also the time to review the structure of how you pay your sales team. Maybe you pay strictly commission based on sales or perhaps you allow a base salary plus a commission of 50%. Whatever your method, now is the time to see if any tweaking can boost profit and boost appeal to the buyer. In case our message is not clear enough yet, we'll say it again: Profitability is everything.

The Clean Books Angle

Keeping good books has never been more important. Even if you have been Johnny-on-the-spot when it comes to record keeping and your books are in tip-top shape, do a fine tooth comb review. Hopefully you have had an upright accountant who has preached that paying taxes is the cost of good business and you have nothing to fear from a buyer's audit. There are still are a couple items lurking in the books that need attention. If you are carrying any bad debts or uncollectibles, now is the time to address that issue. Get the number as low as possible. Do the same for your receivables. Bring accounts receivable as short as you can. Having them sit for 120 days is a deterrent to your buyer. In a perfect world, everyone would pay immediately. We don't live in a perfect world, but 30 days looks so much better than 120 days. Your buyer may not say it out loud, but his inner voice is thinking, "Show me the money."

Now for a moment, let's consider that maybe your books aren't so meticulous and a few things along the way have fallen through the cracks. We're not accusing anyone of anything here, but sometimes, some accountants can suggest many different ways for a business owner to fudge the numbers, show lesser profit, and save on taxes. Now is the time to come clean. Dressing up your business for the sale means showing profit.

It is never too late to turn over a new leaf. However, if a business owner has a history of keeping shady books, he/she may have an extremely difficult time both showing profit when the time comes and convincing a potential buyer that the business is worth the monetary risk.

The first step to take in order to ensure accuracy and cleanliness within your records actually relates to what has been previously discussed. Essentially, you need to get your personal life out of your business. If you have a habit of purchasing things, listing them to your company, and then writing them off, you really need to stop. Unless you find a buyer that lacks any kind of common intuition, you will never sell your business at a fair price – and venture capitalists without vision are exceedingly difficult to come by.

Keep your records as squeaky clean as possible. This simple action will shield you from a great many risks when it comes time for you to sell the business and retire, risks that we will discuss later. If you are concerned that your books are not as accurate as they could be, due either to a history of questionable accounting practices, or just plain old fashioned recognized ignorance, the answer is to seek the aid of an outside CPA. The problem with an in-house accountant is that his/her opinions are usually biased to the point of wild inaccuracy. Outside CPAs are generally more reliable simply because they are not on the payroll. He/she has nothing to gain or lose by the numbers turnout, however promising or not so promising, and is the most qualified representative when it comes to providing you with up-to-date, clean, and trustworthy books.

The above sentence mentions the word "trust" and it is important for us to examine this meaning further. In any business transaction, trust is the most critically important aspect and often the most difficult obstacle to overcome. Not one of the clients or customers that your business has dealt with over the years has handed you money without first convincing him/herself that your products or services, staff, and you yourself were trustworthy. A business that is up for sale is just like any other product or service. If the buyer doesn't trust the value of the business – or you yourself – he/she is not likely to take the risk and write you a check.

Keeping clean books represents trust. If a seller or his/her in-house accountant has been playing games with the financial records over the years, how are they ever to find a buyer who is willing to trust their word on anything? Any company strength that the seller provides will be automatically suspect. Any price offered will likely be denied. The buyer will look at the seller's records and wonder, "If he/she's been lying to the government for all these years, how can I be sure that he/she isn't lying to me?" If you cheat the IRS, your buyer will certainly think you are capable of cheating them.

And what about the flipside? What if the seller manages to find a buyer who looks at the books and still trusts his/her word. Can the seller, in good confidence, trust the buyer? The seller, in truth, can probably expect that the buyer is not the type of buyer and successor that he/she dreamed about. The buyer is probably every bit as untrustworthy as the seller. Most likely, the sale will go through under a contractual agreement – where the buyer provides only a portion of the money required to purchase the business and is contractually bound to pay off the rest over a pre-established period of years. To be certain, "Sold on Contract" are the three dirtiest words that can be applied to the sale of a family business. This is *not* the type of situation that you want to put yourself in – even if the buyer is a member of the family.

The problem with "Sold on Contract" is that it doesn't completely pass responsibility from the seller's hands to the buyer's. In essence, the seller has only sold a portion of the company – and there is absolutely nothing worse than attempting to cut losses by coming out of retirement and fighting to pull a business back out of the tank. In other words, once the business passes from the seller's intellectual control, it stands a fair chance of failing, rendering the business useless and the buyer completely incapable of paying off his/her debt to the seller. "Sold on Contract" has a nasty tendency to destroy a business, curtail a retirement, and lose a great deal of money.

Have an Exit Strategy

Everything we have talked about in this chapter, actually the entire book, is geared toward your exit strategy. Imagine a "12-step" meeting, yet with an altered scenario. "Hi, I'm Bob and I am planning an exit strategy from my business." Applause all around. The first step to solving any problem is to first admit there is a problem. Exiting a business is not a problem per se, but realizing the need to plan for and have an exit strategy is often not part of the mentality of many successful business owners. So much time and energy is spent building and adapting the business, that the final phase of leaving the business sneaks up and can catch the owner unprepared. You, however, are a visionary to the end. The fact that you are holding this book is a prime indicator of your brilliant foresight.

Having an exit strategy is nothing more than taking deliberate steps in order to leave your business on your terms and your schedule. An exit strategy is not a Sunday afternoon epiphany that follows with a Monday morning announcement: Hasta la vista, everyone. The Sunday afternoon epiphany means on Monday morning you start making phone calls to your team of trusted advisors and say, "I read this really great book on succession planning and I want to start getting my ducks in a row now because soon I would like to hand off my beloved business. I know it is a process so let's get started." (We can also provide a really great script on what to say to your spouse when you forget your anniversary.)

Another word for strategy is plan, but strategy sounds more forceful. Maybe it's because we are rugged guys (who sit behind desks all day) that we prefer to say "let's formulate a strategy," but "let's make a plan" works just as well. Regardless of your semantics or your business, you now understand that leaving your business takes time and planning just as starting your business did. Your business didn't happen in an instant and you shouldn't leave it in a hurry either. You are a class act and you will leave your business in style. Leaving in style means leaving your business to the successor you choose, at the time you choose, and hopefully for the price you choose.

Retaining Key Employees (Revisited)

If you recall from two chapters ago, we explored the relevance of keeping your core employees with the business even if they can't imagine working without you. You know they are the backbone of the company's success. Maybe some have been with you since Day One and they take as much pride in the place as you do. A prospective buyer wants an experienced and knowledgeable staff. They are part and parcel of the package deal.

You, being the wise leader, have realized that maybe some employees, family members included, need to switch roles. Matching skills and personalities is a win-win for the company and the staff. You, being the wise leader, understand that it would be very unwise at this point to get rid of the current staff and hire a bunch of minimum wage workers. It might produce a healthy bottom line to dazzle the buyer, but it would severely hurt the business in the long run. Legitimate salaries to qualified workers is not an area to tamper with and a wise buyer knows this fact. You, being the wise leader, also know that a good business is not a one-man show. A smart leader knows how to delegate control. In fact, we bet you could have written the next segment.

Organizing and Delegating Control

We have hinted at this notion already, but it is important to understand that if a business takes a great deal of effort to run on the part of the owner, it is far less valuable to the buyer. This idea is paramount because it is central to both the issue of having an exit strategy and our overall issue of enhancing value for the new buyer. For most family businesses, the solution to this common problem is for the owner to phase out his/her control and responsibility over time. The idea, here, is to make the company as self-sustaining as possible before it comes time to sell.

The goal is to have a veritable sea of buyers. If your business success is because of, or perceived to be because of, you and only you, the future of said business without you looks pretty dismal. Who would want to buy a business that has you as its main asset when that asset is not part of the package deal? That's right, no one.

The nature of your business of course affects the pool of buyers. If you are selling a dental or accounting practice, you will be selling to another professional who has a degree in that field. With other types of businesses, the number of buyers can be limitless. The opportunity to increase the amount of interested parties increases if you are able to show that your business can run without you. If you own a restaurant, it could happen that the dentist has always wanted to run a charming little café like yours. The dentist, in this case, needs to buy an operation that can flow right on, not depending upon you, while he is learning the ropes. Yes, it was your baby and you have lovingly cooked the food, kissed the customers, and cleaned the counters. You have done it all. Now, however, is the time to relax your grip and let your employees do it all. A company that can run itself is what every buyer wants. You will be in a much better position to sell when you can show that the business is not you and you are not Mr. Everything to the business.

If delegating is not your strong point, it is time to learn to let go and let others take the wheel. The ultimate exercise of control is being able to let someone else take over. It is your decision to pass the baton and sell. Now you can stand back and watch with pride as the company and the people you have trained carry on successfully.

Timing, Pricing, and Technology

Let's begin with timing – as the header suggests – and move our way towards technology. Timing is the single most troublesome aspect of selling a business. The fact is that it's almost impossible to know exactly when the buyer is going to become interested and fork over the money. It helps if you're planning to sell to a pre-established successor within the family. At least, then, the discussions about a potential selling date can occur well before you are ready to retire. If you know the timing of the sale, all of the aforementioned steps and strategies to enhance value for the new buyer are easier to carry out.

If you're not planning on selling to a pre-established successor, however, selling a business can sometimes feel a lot like selling a house. You may have to wait for the buyer to weigh his/her options, sell his/her own business – to a buyer who, true to the domino effect, must also wait to sell his/her own business – or generate the kind of cash necessary to invest in the purchase of your company. Knowing this, coupled with the underlying fear that your business may never, in fact, sell at all, it is often more difficult to justify the expenses associated with researching and improving the other two elements outlined in this segment: pricing and technology.

Whatever the case, it is probably in your best interests in both the long- and short-term to invest in research regarding your pricing structure. Why is this? If your business is so outdated that you're still charging the same prices that you were in 1973, then you're still making 1973 profits. Actually, you're making far less than 1973 profits because all of your expenses have managed to appropriately keep up with the times. As simple as this concept may seem, it is a commonly overlooked occurrence among owners of family businesses. Many have scratched their heads trying to figure out why their profits have steadily declined over the past several decades, failing to realize that their only problem was that their products or services were never allowed to proceed in flux with the ever-changing marketplace.

Another aspect to consider is that an inaccurate and far-too-cheap pricing structure may actually be costing you customers/clients. People only pay money for things that they feel are worthwhile. Overly cheap prices tend to carry the connotation of overly cheap products or services. Sometimes, people only buy things *because* they will cost them an adequately large sum of money.

What's worse, if the pricing structure of your company isn't accurate and up-to-date, not only will you see a steady decline in profits over the years, but the business will seem far less attractive to the new buyer. Researching and reestablishing pricing structure takes a great deal of time, money, and effort and, as we've already pointed out, these are three extremely negative words within the typical buyer's mind.

This brings us to the final topic covered within this chapter, certainly a buzzword in today's innovative marketplace: technology.

We've advised you that squeezing as much profit as possible out of your company just before the sale is an excellent strategy for generating more money. This concept does not apply to your investments in new technology. If you have an established schedule for updating your computers or renovating your product production lines, you must stick to it. Cutting corners on your technology investments may produce a healthy bottom line but, unlike some of the other cutbacks we have suggested, it will not make your company seem more attractive to the buyer.

Cutting your technology budget will wound the value of your company in two noteworthy ways. First, although you will be saving a great deal of money in the short-term, you may actually be hurting profits in the long-term. The technologies that you missed out on may make it easier for your competitors to produce products or offer services more quickly and cheaply – causing you to fall generously behind. Secondly, the act of presenting a potential buyer with a company that is technologically outdated is likely to be met with an unfavorable response.

In summary, keeping on par with today's highly-technological world is an absolutely critical effort. Family businesses that fail to meet the technology of their competitors head-on usually find themselves dead in the water. No buyer in his/her right mind would invest in a company that was behind the times. Catching up is far more difficult than keeping up. Cutting your technology budget will only help you to shoot yourself in the foot – both before and during the selling process.

~~~

No matter what you decide – no matter how profound and informative this chapter may have been – there is nothing that you can do to ensure that your asking price is equivalent to the price offered by the buyer. At the outset, the number in your head is likely to be much higher than the number in the buyer's. The final, and perhaps the only, true method to getting as much money as possible out of the sale is to employ good old fashioned iron-fisted negotiation. Hiring a business broker and a team of outside consultants to help you prove the worth of your business would be well within your best interests.

Chapter 10

Financing the Transition

As you bid a fond farewell to your glory days as the family business patriarch/matriarch, either reluctantly or eagerly, you cross the threshold into the next era of your life. Congratulations, the phase you are about to enter is what advertisers refer to as your "golden years". The sun shines brightly everyday, your teeth are perfectly white, you have no lower back pain, and you can play tennis or with the grandchildren. With or without a nagging backache, you no doubt have many plans about how to spend life's most precious asset: your time. Make no mistake, those plans also most certainly need another asset behind them: cash.

Once the decision is made to sell, most business owners mistakenly believe that they can get a check one day and they're out the door with a hearty handshake and a skip in their step. Make note: This almost *never* happens. Very few deals are made for all cash.

In a perfect world, you would hand over the keys in exchange for a big fat lump sum and be on your merry way. But as you know from all these years in business, we don't live in a perfect world. Many business owners have to carry at least a small part of the business, depending upon how badly they want to sell it. It is very difficult to have an all or none sale.

In response, many different workarounds have been developed in the industry. Let's take the time to examine some of the more common ones. Hopefully, at least one method suits your needs – that way you can look forward to selling your business and still having sufficient cash flow to take the grandkids to Disney World or cruise the Panama Canal.

70/20/10

The title of this segment may look like the title of a new drama on Fox, but it's actually a rather stringent rule when it comes to selling a business. The 70/20/10 rule in today's market means 70% bank financing, 20% down payment from your buyer, and 10% on an installment or balloon payment. As the owner, this may not be the most attractive method because you are still largely on the hook with the bank. Most owners want the sale to be complete, fini, finito, terminado. Ideally, you, the seller, would be gone, on the beach reading a stack of best sellers or backpacking in the Himalayas or perhaps just meticulously arranging your millions in precise rows in your sock drawer. The fact of the matter is, however, that most buyers do not have the capability to fund the transaction in one fell swoop.

If you are selling your business to your child, you may of course be prepared for some financial ties and never expected to deal and dash, anyway. It may never have been your plan to sail off into the sunset with nary a backward glance. If sticking around is more your style, this 70/20/10 arrangement is much easier to swallow.

Angel Investors

What happens quite often in the sale of business, to a family member or an unrelated party, is the funding comes from what is referred to as an angel investor. It is very common that the interested party who wants to buy the business is short on funds. This buyer, maybe even your child, seeks out a wealthy friend or relative and asks for a little help in the form of a loan. You, the family business owner and the one selling out, could indeed very well be that relative helping out your son or daughter by acting as angel investor. Like we've said before, small business owners wear many hats. Sometimes it's the occasional halo.

Usually the angel investor or investors is no more than one or two people that are associated with the buyer. Maybe your daughter had a college roommate who hit it big in the home candle party market and is willing to lend her some money to take over your family business. The angel investor is not in it for the long term and usually wants to get out of the deal within three to five years. The angel is hoping for some rate of return, but being an angel after all, is not interested in becoming part of the management of the company or exerting any influence in how things are run. It's as close to a no-strings relationship as we see in financial dealings.

An investor of this category usually knows the buyer and is willing to take a chance, but with calculated risk. Even angel investors don't foolishly throw their money away, bringing to mind the old saying: Only fools rush in where angels fear to tread.

Angel investors serve as the financial backer and oftentimes a psychological show of support. If Uncle Fred fronts the money to your son Freddy, it is his way of showing his confidence in Freddy's ability to take over the business and run the show – and probably a nice big thank you to you for naming your kid after him in the first place. Whatever the case, angel investors tend to believe in the project and the person they are investing in. They have the deep pockets to help someone they love eventually develop the deep pockets as well and maybe even become an angel investor for the next in line in future generations.

Venture Capital

Maybe your buyer is very capable to take over the operations, but short on dough – nd all their friends and relatives are tapped out too. Not everyone has an angel investor to turn to or a fairy godmother with a magic wand. Instead they may choose to find a venture capitalist.

Using a venture capital firm is a common method employed to finance such transactions. Maybe your son wants to buy your business, but does not have the necessary resources on his own. He may have been hoping Uncle Fred would back him, but unbeknownst to the family, Uncle Fred lost his life savings in the Beanie Baby craze a few years back. Even with no angel on his shoulder, your son can easily find a venture capital firm through a business broker, his CPA or business attorney, his bank or brokerage firm, or of course, by using man's best friend, the internet.

Venture capitalists are usually a group of investors with money to burn. Actually, perhaps that's a bit too nonchalant as far as descriptions go. To revise: They are outsiders using outside money. These investors are typically not related and have no intimate relationship with the buyer, the seller, or the business. They are wealthy individuals looking to finance the transition of your business sale in the hopes of increasing their pile of pennies. Helping out the buyer is not their motivation. Venture capitalists enter into a business venture having capital in order to make capital. They adhere to the old adage, "you have to spend money to make money". They normally want to be involved for 3 to 5 years and it is not out of the ordinary that they may wish to be actively involved in management.

A venture capital group is a pre-assembled incorporation with pre-assembled dollars. There may be a group of 200 people with $1 million or more to invest. The person in charge takes all that capital and buys companies, hoping to build a conglomerate that could become worth even more money in three to five years.

Of course, it should be noted that venture capitalists are sometimes referred to as "vulture capitalists". This rather unflattering term is derived from the idea that the seller of a business or the buyer lacking funds sometimes find themselves so desperate for funds that they are left vulnerable enough for the vultures to swoop in for the kill. The venture capitalists care very little for sentimentality. They're only in it for the numbers and dollars.

Private Equity Groups

Another option for the cash-strapped buyer looking for funds to finance the deal is to use what is called a private equity group (PEG). Sometimes the terms "private equity" groups and "venture capital" groups are used interchangeably, but they *are* different.

A private equity group is a conglomerate of investors who are using their own money. They are not the movers and shakers of the venture capitalist arena. Typically, the buyer knows at least one of the investors. Maybe your daughter is ready and willing to be your successor. Perhaps her husband's cousin and his three best friends are looking for a little more action than their weekly poker night. They believe that your successful business and your intelligent daughter are a winning combination and they are willing to go all in. Their investment is not a silent partnership or a gift, however – they want to be involved in the management; and they want to keep their hand in it for the long haul.

Let's say your business is Papa's Pie Shop. Your daughter, still Daddy's Little Girl in your eyes, has the business acumen of Mrs. Fields, Auntie Anne, and Gloria Jean all rolled up into one dynamite businesswoman. She's been running the place since she was a teenager. Now that you are ready to turn in your rolling pin, she will take the business to new heights and her private equity group will fly high right alongside her. They will stay involved forever, enjoying their piece of the pie.

Bank Financing

Don't worry, we didn't forget good old fashioned bank financing. Sometimes the old tried and true way works best. A person, be it your family member or not, in the position to buy a business should already have a good long-term relationship established with their banker. That business banker, as such, will be more than willing to work out the terms of a loan to help buy the family dream.

Oftentimes, business loans are supported by the Small Business Administration. The SBA usually will only get involved up to $3 million, however. They are more like a guarantor for the bank. The true mission of the SBA is to create jobs, and if they can do that by guaranteeing loans, then they're essentially fulfilling their goal *and* helping out the buyer of the business. Everybody wins. Because the job factor is the underlying motivation of the SBA, however, there is a natural bias toward companies with a relatively large number of employees.

Maybe the business you are selling is small and with few employees. Your son has proven himself the rightful successor, but as is normal, he does not have the cash flow to buy you out. Suppose you don't have the liquid resources to be his angel investor or maybe he simply doesn't want you to be. He wants to do it on his own. The option of bank financing can be a good one and honestly is the method most often used to finance the transition of a family business to the next leader.

Closing the Deal

There are several ways to finance the transition. Your buyer – be it a family member or an outside party – and you, as the seller, will achieve a mutually satisfactory arrangement. You have presented your business in the best light possible. It is spiffed and shined and ready to roll. You feel pride and a bittersweet tear forms in the corner of your eye. You are secure in the sales price because you wisely sought the expert valuation of an independent business appraiser. No matter what method of financing is used, your buyer and any lender involved will be much easier to deal with – and will feel secure as well – knowing that the business was appraised by an unbiased professional.

It's now smooth sailing straight ahead. Onward and upward. Off into the sunset. What other clichés can we throw at you? How about the one that nothing is certain in life but death and taxes. No matter how you package the deal, Uncle Sam is not going to be left out of the party. How much cake he is going to take and how can you control the size of his piece? Stick around and find out. We promise the next chapter, although it discusses taxes, will not put you to sleep.

Chapter 11

Tax Strategies and Charitable Planning

How serendipitous is it that our chapter on tax strategies carries the same number as the most notorious bankruptcy clam? Hopefully, the employ of the strategies within this so-named chapter will help you and your successor to avoid such a rough condition.

Let us suppose for an instant that the previous chapter did not interest you. We do not doubt our ability to have you riveted to every word, but perhaps the content of the Financing the Transition simply did not apply. If that's the case, you skimmed right through it because you have known all along that *you* would be the one financing the transition. Your father helped you out financially when you took over leadership of the family business and it has always been your intention to help your offspring when it is their turn to take the helm. If that is case, then we are glad we saved the juicy stuff for this chapter.

You, the owner, must use the fair market value derived by the independent appraiser as your selling price and you must use the established interest rate on the loan to your loved one for the transaction to be deemed legitimate and not be construed as a gift in the eyes of the IRS. And oh, what far reaching and questioning eyes they have.

Congratulate yourself – you've done the tough stuff. You've chosen a proper successor and sufficiently trained him/her. You've communicated so much with your family and employees that you feel like you could be the next Dr. Phil. The timing is right and you feel comfortable stepping aside. But before you pack your bags for the Parcheesi™ playoffs, you still have the Internal Revenue Service to contend with.

If you are of certain age, you may recall the old Steve Martin comedy bit. He explains that he knows the secret of how to make a million dollars and never pay taxes: First, get a million dollars. Second, when the IRS calls you up and asks about the taxes, you simply say, "I forgot!" If it were that easy, we would not be experiencing the joy of sharing our profound knowledge with you. Always remember, we're here to help.

Charitable Remainder Trusts

The first item we want to tell you about is called a *Charitable Remainder Trust*. This is a special type of arrangement in which property or money is donated to a charity (that's the charitable part), but the donor continues to use the property and/or receive income from it while living (that's the remainder part). You, the donor, avoid any capital gain tax on the donated assets, and you also get an income tax deduction for the fair market value of the remainder interest that the trust earned. The real beauty is that the asset is removed from your taxable estate, reducing subsequent estate taxes. If you recall from Chapter 3 on Estate Planning Issues, estate taxes can account for a substantial chunk of change.

A charitable remainder trust can be an excellent vehicle to use to transfer the closely held stock of your business. Because dividends are not often paid on the stock and the charity may not be able to sell the stock (and you don't want a stranger as an owner in your company anyway), one sophisticated technique is to have the charity sell the stock back to the company. That way, they have the proceeds to invest. Very clever indeed.

There are three types of charitable remainder trusts: a charitable remainder annuity trust (CRAT), a charitable remainder unitrust (CRUT), and a pooled income trust. We'll spare you the nitty gritty details of each, but your financial advisors and estate tax planners can steer you in the right direction.

Installment sales

One strategy for realizing the full price of the sale of the business while deferring – and possibly lowering one's tax consequences – is the installment sale. An installment sale is a strategy under which the seller of the business receives the full compensation for the business over a number of years, thus allowing him/her to be taxed only on the amount of the sale's price received in that given year.

Until October 18th, 2006, the PAT – it this case, the acronym refers to Private Annuity Trust, rather than Point After Try – and the Deferred Sales Trust (DST) were two favored techniques of implementing an installment sale. Unfortunately, on the 18th, the IRS put forth a proposed regulation stating that it would no longer recognize the deferred tax treatment of an installment sale by way of a PAT or DST. While this was only proposed, it had a chilling effect on the use of these techniques as the IRS only gave a 24-hour notice window for implementation of such devices. What this really meant was that any PAT or DST entered into after that date would not receive the tax deferral treatment if the proposed regulation was actually placed into effect. Since IRS-proposed regulations are normally accepted, all attorneys, accountants, and financial advisors were put on notice that the PAT and the DST were effectually ineffective for this purpose.

Did this mean that installment sales were dead as a tax deferral tool? Absolutely not. We wouldn't be writing about it if it weren't relevant. There are still several ways to implement an installment sale independent of the DST or even without tacking on the PAT. Call it a two-point conversion. The simplest way is to draft the purchase agreement so that the seller carries a promissory note in which he/she will receive a portion of the sales price as a down payment and the remainder over a period of years with interest.

For example, Sally sells her business to Brian for $1 million. At the time that the sale closes, Brian pays Sally $500,000 and then signs a promissory note for the remaining amount to be paid out over ten years with an interest rate of 7%. Sally would be taxed on the $500,000 received in the first year and would be taxed on only $50,000 per year for the next ten years. The interest she received would be taxed as income rather than capital gains.

A less formal way to set up an installment sale is to create a consulting agreement in which much of the sales price is allocated towards paying the seller for consulting rather than as part of the sale. If we use the above example, we might structure it so that Sally receives $500,000 as the full payment for the business at the time of closing, but that she would also receive $100,000 per year for five years for consulting services to Brian. It is important to note that Sally would not pay capital gains on the $100,000 installments. Instead, she would pay the much simpler (and far less costly) employment-related taxes and income taxes.

When trying to determine whether an installment sale is appropriate for you (and what the benefits and consequences will be with each possible technique), it is critical that you consult a good corporate attorney, CPA, and/or financial advisor as all installment sales techniques have their own specific tax and legal ramifications. Failure to set them up correctly, after all, can lead to tax troubles down the road.

ESOP

Let's move on to one of our favorite strategies for the transition of your business: the ESOP. No, we're not talking about the ancient Greek author of fables. That was Aesop. In this case, an ESOP is an *Employee Stock Ownership Plan* and we are firm believers in them. Such a plan helps you get top dollar for your business, and with your employees as the buyers, morale tends to be very high. It's a bona fide win-win.

An ESOP is a type of qualified employee retirement benefit plan that allows the company's employees to participate in the ownership of company stock through the plan. Clear as mud? The first and most obvious rule – it is the *employee* stock ownership plan, after all – is that in order to establish an ESOP for your company, you must have employees. Plural. A one-man corporation cannot hop on an ESOP. The second buzzword is stock. Partnerships and proprietorships don't have stock, so therefore, no ESOP.

Two common uses of ESOPs are to provide an employee retirement benefit tied to the value of the company's stock and to provide a buyer for the owner's stock of a closely held business. ESOPs are highly regulated by the Internal Revenue Code and the Employment Retirement Income Security Act of 1974 (ERISA). Okay, they don't have the flexibility of the aforementioned installment plans, but they offer significant tax advantages that make them worthwhile. It's been a couple paragraphs since we last said it: we strongly recommend you seek the consult of an experienced attorney.

Proponents of ESOPs maintain that they create improved productivity among employees because the staff realizes that their ultimate retirement benefit may be greatly enhanced if the company does well. It is in the employee's best interest to help insure the company's overall success. They now truly have a vested interest and they are not just working solely for their weekly take-home pay. It does make sense that there is added initiative in a job well done.

Another plus to the ESOP is that employees are not taxed until the shares are distributed. Any appreciation of the stock held in the plan is not taxed to employees when they receive their distribution. Taxation on the unrealized appreciation will not happen until the shares are sold by the employee which we can assume is in their retirement years when they are in a lower tax bracket.

Plan allocation formulas must not discriminate in favor of highly compensated employees. They are typically based on employee compensation. For example, if total payroll is $500,000 and the employer contributes stock worth $50,000, an employee earning $10,000 would be allocated $1,000 worth of stock.

ESOPs are designed to invest their assets in the company stock rather than investing in the public markets. Annual cash contributions are made to the ESOP. The ESOP then purchases stock from the company or the company may contribute the stock directly. In either case, the company gets a tax deduction for the value of the contribution each year while the cash stays with the company. A cash contribution is returned to the company through the purchase of company stock and the direct stock contribution does not involve cash at all so an ESOP results in an annual cashless deduction for the company. Makes you want to yell BINGO! This card's a winner.

ESOPs, unlike all other qualified retirement plans, are permitted to borrow money for the purpose of purchasing company stock. When the ESOP borrows funds to buy stock, the company makes annual contributions to the ESOP in the amount equal to the ESOP's principal and interest payments on the loan. The ESOP then uses the contributions to pay back that debt service. Since the company's contribution as a whole is deductible, that makes the interest and the principal on the loan deductible. In addition to borrowing from the company itself, an ESOP may also borrow from an owner of the company who wants to sell.

Selling your business to an ESOP may be the perfect solution for you and your business. An ESOP may represent a ready buyer. Besides serving the purpose of being an incentive and benefit for your employees, it also has the unique ability to borrow, which can make it a potential buyer when you are ready to retire. You would be leaving your legacy in the very hands that helped shape it. It is a pretty enticing package for all involved.

Sometimes, in all our ramblings, we forget this chapter is supposed to tackle tax issues. The sale of your business to an ESOP can provide you with tax advantages. The most significant factor occurs when you sell your stock to the ESOP and the ESOP owns at least 30 percent of the company after the sale. You are then allowed to defer the tax on your gain on the sale by reinvesting the proceeds you receive in qualified replacement property – which is IRS-speak for "certain domestic U.S. securities". If you hold the replacement securities until you die, then as a result of estate tax rules that give the securities a stepped-up basis, no tax is thus ever paid on the original gain.

We like the words "defer tax"; we love the words "no tax." That little precious piece of tax law is a very powerful motivation for you to sell your interest in your closely held business to an ESOP potentially tax free instead of to another buyer off the street. Allow us to provide an example:

Martin originally invested $200,000 in his closely held business and those shares are now worth $2 million. Kudos to Martin. Martin is ready to fulfill his lifelong dream of climbing Mt. Kilimanjaro and has a prospective buyer. Assuming a combined federal and state income tax rate of 32%, Martin would rake in proceeds of $1,360,000 and would be subject to taxes of $640,000 if he sold to this buyer. If he sold to an ESOP and reinvested his $2,000,000 in qualifying securities, Martin would be subject to $0 in federal income taxes on the sale. *No tax on the sale*. It's a beautiful thing.

But beauty is not without its stipulations. There are conditions, of course, for selling to an ESOP. For example, your holding period in the stock must be at least three years. The ESOP must own at least 30% of the company immediately after the sale. Private companies are required to have an annual outside valuation to determine the price of their shares. We'll spare you the rest of the details, but be aware that you must file an election statement with the Internal Revenue Service and always, always, always consult your trusted advisors.

Let's Get Charitable

Now that we are practically breathless and giddy, let's chat about charity, another favorite subject. As we have stated earlier, regular charitable giving is, for lack of a better word, good. You have been successful and giving back to your community is a nice thank you gesture. Maybe you have a cause you believe in and now that you have a little spare change, nothing warms your heart more than donating to an organization whose mission you believe very strongly in. There is always the chance that you are the original Ebenezer Scrooge, before he was visited by Marley and the Christmas ghosts and you are not motivated by goodwill. But, either way, you have to agree though – it is good business to be a good giver.

There are many benefits in regular gifting to charities. In addition to the fact that you can live to see your money being used to improve your local, state, national, or world community or, on your death, by providing for charitable donations in your will, you can know that you have completed a generous act post mortem. And, Ebenezer, the act of charitable giving also provides income and estate tax breaks for both you and your beneficiaries.

In order to flesh out the positives of charitable giving more completely, we provide this list. Charitable giving:

- Supplies the donor with a sense of satisfaction knowing that his/her money is being put to good use by the charity.

There is perhaps no greater pleasure than knowing that you've done something meaningful for someone else – that you've given back to a community that has given so much to you. Try it. You might find it highly addictive.

- Gifts given during the lifetime of the donor can significantly reduce his/her income tax liability.

Don't care about the personal gratification associated with giving? How about the tax breaks? Another great benefit to gifting is that you can write it off. This is simply because charitable giving is a willful act to part with a portion of one's assets. Give and you shall receive. If nothing else, think of the act of charity as giving away a great deal of tax liability.

- Appreciable gifts given during the lifetime of the donor can significantly reduce his/her estate tax liability.

Just like with income tax, charitable giving can decrease your estate tax liability. If valuable property or any other kind of appreciable asset is gifted to a charity, it is taken out of your hands and, therefore, untaxable. The estate tax return allows for a charitable deduction: If the decedent leaves property to a qualifying charity, it is deductible from the gross estate. Double benefit: The charities of your choice receive a donation and your heirs have a reduced estate tax burden.

- Giving does a great deal of good for society.

And the best part is that you are in complete control of where your money goes and what it is used for. You may wish to guide your money, during your lifetime, to be used in researching the cure for cancer. Or, upon your death, you may stipulate within your will that a portion of your estate is to be used to improve your Alma Mater or advance stem cell research. Make your presence felt.

From a tax standpoint, charitable contributions result in a trifecta: they are a current income tax deduction, they can reduce estate taxes, and they can be made free of gift tax. Sometimes overlooked, however, is the need for the organization to be "qualified." You may believe your favorite agency is qualified to receive your dollars and qualified to give you a tax deduction, but it is a wise precaution to double check.

The Internal Revenue Service publishes a list of qualified charities in IRS Publication 78 and your organization of choice should be able to provide you with a 501(c) letter that verifies their charitable status. Remember that a contribution to an individual is never deductible. Non-cash contributions are subject to a qualified appraisal in order to arrive at the value allowed as a deduction.

A gift to charity is probably one of the simplest estate planning techniques. During your lifetime, charitable giving can be accomplished merely by writing a check, assigning stock, transferring life insurance policies, signing a deed to real estate, or conveying property in any other outright manner. Likewise, at death, gifts to charity can be made by will, by life insurance contract, by employee benefit contract (the death benefits from a pension plan can be paid to charity), or by trust.

No matter the size of the gift, you will never be liable for gift tax on charitable contributions to a qualified charity. The organization will not have to pay any tax on receipt and generally no tax on income generated by the donated property. Charitable organizations are all feeling the brunt of declining donations. If you feel compelled to give, do it now and do it again at death.

Perhaps the wildest bit of advice we can offer: Gifts to charitable organizations can reduce your federal estate tax – the amount of the deduction is the amount of the gift. You can leave your entire estate to charity and a deduction will be allowed for the entire gift. Although we respect such benevolence, you better discuss that one with your family.

~~~

We could wax on and on, but we know you have devoured these eleven chapters and are ready to top it off with the final chapter. After you digest everything you have read, you need to act. Take a walk. Think, but don't stew. Maybe when you first opened the book, the whole idea of succession planning seemed a little overwhelming. Maybe the very notion of leaving behind your business is the real culprit. Your business is the success that it is because you have done the right thing at the right time. If now is not the time to turn in your Superman cape, it is certainly the right time to start the plan in motion. Remember the title of this book is Succession Planning, not Jump Ship Today. A good plan is all you need and now you have the tools to get the ball rolling. How fast you want the ball to roll is up to you.

Section 5:
What Now?

Chapter 12

Remember, You Sold It...
Or Did You?

Is it sunrise or sunset in your life? This question might just be hackneyed enough to be found on the inside of a Hallmark card, but corny though it may be, it's among the first questions that you must ask yourself as you embark upon that simultaneously most sought-after and most dreaded phase of your life – retirement. It's tantamount to picking out what you will have for breakfast on your first morning of freedom or deciding if you will play 18 or 36 holes of golf. Or perhaps, if we can be allowed to take a slightly more serious approach to the question, it should be wrapped up in your decision on where to retire, what kind of home you'll be living in, and what on earth you plan on doing with all that free time.

The sunrise/sunset metaphor also points to the question of what to do with all that money you just made during the sale. Is it enough to carry you through your 90's? Make no mistake, a great many people are living at least that long these days. Will you over-save, bringing about a decline in the lifestyle to which you've grown accustomed? Will you overspend, allowing your hard-earned nest egg to fizzle before you even have the chance to pass it to your children and grandchildren? Is there a middle ground that affords personal comfort for now and the future?

You've made it through the most difficult passage of a business owner's life – preparing for and completing the sale of something you've worked so hard to build and maintain – but that doesn't mean you're in the clear. Far too many people hold the words "retirement" and "funeral" in similar regard. We call these people "sunset people." If our goal is to instruct you on how to successfully and happily pass your business on to the next generation – and the chapters you've already read should have suggested that this is, in fact, our goal – then we would be remiss if we didn't suggest that, upon the day of your retirement (and, indeed, long before it), you must take a step back and consider the strategies you'll employ in order to become one of the "sunrise people." You can be one of those people that look upon the remaining decades of your life as an opportunity for personal gain despite the lack of professional fulfillment to which you've grown so accustomed.

For many people, the prospect of decades without work can seem rather terrifying. After all, there is only so much golf that can be played. We are here to tell you that there's a great big world out there and you, the successful former-owner and now seller of a family business, have the means to experience it to its fullest without breaking the bank. Furthermore, there may be ways for you to stay somewhat involved with your business despite your retirement and despite its passage to new ownership. It's just a matter of working out which level of involvement is best for you (and your company).

Selling Points

To be certain, there are any number of ways to sell a business – any number of benefits to owner or seller, tax strategies, ownership structures, and financing streams – and all of them work to influence just what kind of life you'll lead in retirement (and, most likely, what kind of chance your business will have to survive once you're gone). The possibilities are as numerous as legal creativity is wide – and anyone that has ever had the pleasure of meeting a good lawyer is right to be intimidated by this thought. To save both your time and our page-space, we will discuss only two of the most broadly-defined and widely-employed methods of sale: Cash Sale and Sold-on-Contract.

If we can be allowed room for procrastination, we'll start with the simpler of the two methods. A Cash Sale is pretty much exactly what it sounds like (except, very rarely are large briefcases filled with unmarked $20 bills involved). What this method refers to is the simple act of a buyer working to scrape together the funds necessary to buy the company from you outright. Its greatest benefit is that you can rest easy knowing that (assuming that you utilized an appraiser to properly assess the value of your business) you've maximized the amount of money you could have possibly received from the sale. Its drawbacks are twofold: 1) You can and should no longer take part in the direction of your business and 2) Unless you have a creative and thoughtful money manager (and, ahem, we can think of a few) the sale of your business could represent the very last significant paycheck that you will ever receive. Despite these drawbacks, this strategy is right for most people – especially those that sell to family members – and most businesses.

Sold-On-Contract. Ah, hear the clarion call of this most misunderstood of methods. Basically, this means that the business is sold based on certain performance milestones or certain executive decisions made (somewhere down the road) on the part of the buyer or seller. The ownership of the company changes hands but the original owner is allowed to stay on until things seem to be going smoothly enough for him/her to step down. This method of sale might seem particularly attractive to any number of sellers: Those with a business whose profitability occasionally wavers, those that feel their business couldn't possibly succeed without them, those that run into buyers who may be a little short on scratch, and those that, other than actively take part in the advancement of their company, simply cannot think of anything constructive to do during retirement (more on this type of person later in the chapter).

The attraction is an honest one. Sold-on-Contract may seem to provide both seller and buyer an enhanced sense of flexibility in lieu of cash. It might seem to actively provide both the new owner with a period of tutorial and the departing owner with something to do to fill the hours of retirement. Everybody wins, right? Most often, no. The trouble with Sold-on-Contract is that it quite often represents the potential for dispute and inevitably leads to an all-out power struggle – neither of which is particularly advisable for a family business, since they are liable to infect the harmony of both the business and the family.

The other problem with Sold-on-Contract is that, whenever a bank becomes involved (as they inevitably do when such a significant transaction occurs) this method of sale tends to keep the seller on the hook. What's the trouble with this? Imagine for a moment that, after you step down as full-capacity leader, your business begins to falter and there's nothing you can do to get it back on track. You could potentially wind up with as much as 50% of the liability for the money lost. What if the buyer has taken out a loan to help finance the transition and then, due to the failure of the company, cannot pay his/her debts? The answer is terrifying even to write about: The aging business owner, near his/her retirement, is left with both a staggering debt and a bad-apple business. The financial implications would be crippling. If you're considering employing the Sold-on-Contract method of sale, be sure to consult a good financial consultant and/or lawyer. The method represents shaky ground, to be certain. Never forget that if things should go awry, banks aren't often willing to allow you to simply walk away.

Emotion

We would be kidding ourselves if we believed that it will be easy for you to just walk away from your business. It's like a child to you, we know. The fact remains, however, that, after you've done all your work and your heir-apparent steps in (at some point), you have to stop running the company. Very few tribes have two chiefs.

Then you become faced with the ridiculous amount of free time that you now have to fill. Ask yourself if you are emotionally prepared to transition from your 40 years of working 60-hour weeks to the prospect of 0-hour weeks. Thinking back on all the time you've spent at work can be rather off-putting, to be certain. Over the years, what you do for a living likely has managed to become an indelible part of your identity. Are you ready for such a significant change?

Being not just a business owner, but the owner of a family business puts you at an advantage when considering the emotions associated with the sale. Selling to a family member has its perks. For one, the buyer most likely cares a great deal about you and your well-being. This factor will probably contribute to a greater sense of flexibility when it comes to the topic of you sticking around (in some capacity) to help the company. As long as you're willing to hang up your spurs as the outright leader of the business (and you must be careful not to cross any lines), the following two scenarios are perfectly capable of aiding you in your quest to fill free time and aiding your successor in his/her quest to keep the company moving forward:

1.   Stay on as a consultant.

So, the family business has its flaws after all. Imagine that your successor runs into a problem that he/she doesn't know how to solve on his/her own. Rather than hire an outside consultant (and spend good company money to do it), why not turn to the expert? Your successor could span the globe in search of that jack-of-all-trades consultant with the proper industry knowledge, but why would he/she do that when the perfect candidate for the job is right there to help?

This scenario has its advantages. First off, it's tailor-made for your strengths. You're a business owner – solving problems is your specialty. It also has the dual benefit of occasionally giving you something to do while not requiring that you stay on as a full time employee. You'd become something of an outside contractor with inside knowledge – a resource that your successor could use whenever in trouble – and that is exactly the kind of aid and expertise a company in transition will need.

2.   Take a permanent seat on a board of directors.

There. In this scenario, you haven't stepped down entirely. You also haven't rescinded all of your power. Basically, under these circumstances, you relinquish your power of veto and simply take up the power of the vote. You move from President to Senator – and, as far as power is concerned, we can think of worse moves.

You'll have something to prepare for and something to do (hence, many hours to fill) every time the board meets. These meetings can be as often as weekly or as rare as quarterly. Just make sure that, whatever the decision on how to structure the board, it is a consensus one – and that both you and your successor have each had your say in how to set things up.

Much like the consulting role, being on a board is not necessarily a full-time position. You'll be able to maintain a guiding interest without bogging yourself down too much or risk becoming an overbearing presence to your successor. Unlike the consulting role, your responsibilities (and boundaries) will be clearly defined by a charter or contract that will be drawn up in advance of the board's first assembly.

Boredom et al.

You did it, you've retired. If neither of the above scenarios regarding maintaining an active part in your business appeal to you, what do you do now? The next expanse of years stretch out ahead of you. Recall the parable of the elderly farmer that sells his land and moves into the city. Without plowing and planting, he can think of little to do. As a result, his health declines and he dies sooner than anyone would have imagined. It's a bleak story – but one with a moral: if you want to stay healthy and happy, you need to be creative about ways to maintain the level of mental (or, in the case of the farmer, physical) activity to which you've grown accustomed.

Another question that is every bit as important to ask is, how do you sustain your nest-egg? Sure, you're more loaded than you've ever been in your life, but how can you gauge both how long your life will be and how much money it will take for you to live comfortably?

In answer to the first predicament (that of filling your time and keeping your mind stimulated), we offer a few potential solutions:

- Pursue your lifelong dream.

Have you ever wanted to travel the world? Run a marathon? Own a pub? Now's your chance. With the kind of time, money, and motivation that you now have in your possession, any and all of these dreams can be pursued. It's never too late to check things off your lifelong to-do list.

- Give back.

You've led a successful life. You've been granted a lot of opportunities that many people in your community (and across the world) have not. In fact, without the patronage of these same people, you might not have had a profitable business in the first place. Perhaps you should use your newfound free time to give back to the community that has given you so much over the years. And, if that's not enough to motivate you, take this into consideration: studies show that volunteering 1 hour of your time per week could add 10 years to your life.

- Get creative.

Write a book. Paint your masterpiece. Take up woodworking. There are as many hobbies and pastimes as there are retirees in this country. You may think that creativity isn't your thing – but how would you know? You've been working 60-hour weeks your whole life. You may have talents that you never even had time to realize.

- Fulfill a fancy.

Maybe you have a secret desire that doesn't fall into the category of a lifelong dream, but just one of those things you've been saving for "some day." That someday is here. As a business owner, you are no stranger to risk. Now you can be a thrill seeker. Want to feel the rush of jumping out of a plane? Go for it; with proper instruction and a parachute, of course. Always harbored a hankering to pilot a hot-air balloon over wine country for an afternoon? You can. You now have the time and the money to indulge a whim or two. Perhaps you've been promising your spouse for two decades that you would take ballroom dance lessons. This is your golden opportunity, Twinkle Toes. The possibilities are as limitless and as individual as you are. All those times over the years when you told yourself, "Some day I'd like to try that," now you can. The world lies before you to explore and enjoy.

Now when you ask yourself that question, (What will I do now?), we hope your eyes are bright with anticipation, that your list is a mile long, and that you're excited to get started.

The Never-Ending Nest-Egg

Okay, you are pumped up and ready to face retirement with youthful fervor, but the second predicament has now crossed your mind – will the money last? Everyone heading into this phase of life wants to be sure that their savings and the proceeds from the sale of the business will sustain them through the rest of their lives. Increased longevity and volatile financial markets may raise concerns among retirees that they may down the road find themselves in a diminished dollar circumstance. No one wants to end up in the poorhouse, but you don't need to live the life of a pauper to avoid that perilous end. Even if you live to be a hundred and one, or older, you can outlive your assets. You are not alone if you wonder how much can be withdrawn each year without depleting your holdings. You can maintain a comfortable lifestyle, keep up with inflation, and not run out of money. Some people spend a lot of time configuring retirement portfolios to hedge market risk when they should be more concerned about maintaining income levels for life. This is the part where we toot our own horn and tell you: we're here to help.

Maybe you feel a panic attack coming on when you realize you have not lived below your means and have not built up a nest egg equal to 25 times your annual spending. Don't panic. No worries. The first five years of retirement is usually the most expensive. You break free from the daily grind and travel and indulge yourself. This is 100% normal and actually well-deserved after a long career. You don't need to feel guilt or retiree's remorse. Enjoy yourself. You can rest assured knowing that household expenditures do in fact decline as retirees age. You won't be spending like a crazy person year after year after year. Statistics show that in later years, spending usually drops dramatically. Every person is unique and there are many variables to consider of course. The inverse relationship between age at retirement and spending has implications for financial planning obviously. Some folks want to retire at 55; some are still going strong at work until age 75. Whatever your situation is, you need to discuss your needs and wants with a trusted financial advisor who can assess what is the best strategy for you and your hard earned nest egg. It is wise to put your eggs in more than one basket. Meet with your financial planner to pick what baskets work best for your eggs.

And Now...The Rest of the Story

Actually, the rest of the story is yours to write. We have presented a wealth of information aimed to preserve your wealth and that of your company. And we hope to preserve your sanity, too. Owning a family business is perhaps one of the most difficult vocations on the planet. Selling a family business can be downright overwhelming. There are many factors to consider. If you've forgotten already, we have discussed the six dangerous D's that can threaten your business;

we touched on estate planning and asset protection; we have convinced you that nothing can happen successfully without family communication; we offered guidance on selecting your successor and retaining key employees; we've covered your business worth, enhancing its value, financing the transition, and tax strategies and charitable planning. Frankly, we're exhausted.

There is a lot of important material in these pages. You are wise to be holding this book because as we stated in the first chapter, he who hesitates is lost. Succession planning – in the words of a six-year-old or a sixty-year-old – could be described as "no fun". That may be true, but then again, we believe that planning for the future is always exciting. A philosopher, or maybe it was a bumper sticker, once said: Never is life so exciting as at the beginning of a journey.

Before you begin this next journey, please remember our repeated disclaimer. Man cannot live on bread alone and man cannot successfully pass his company to the next generation alone. Consult your team of trusted financial advisors as you map out your blueprint for the future. They will keep you aware of the latest tax changes and challenges and how to plan accordingly. Even if your retirement is still several years away, begin the planning process now. You will be glad you did. It took you decades to build your successful business and it will likewise take time to manage the transition successfully. You have blazed trails that your successor can follow and, more importantly, you have taught your next line of leaders how to blaze their own trails.

A Chinese proverb states: What you cannot avoid, welcome. Succession planning cannot be avoided, so welcome this new challenge as you have all the other challenges you've faced throughout your career. The golden and glorious years of retirement await you and it is our sincere wish that you welcome and embrace the opportunities that now lay before you. Vienna waits for you. Volunteering waits for you. Variegated petunias in the garden wait for you. Or maybe a late-night screening of *The Godfather* in your living room waits for you. Whatever your whim, wish, or want, we hope you see that there is a beautiful sunrise on the horizon. And we hope that you see that the time for succession planning is now.

About the Authors

Mike Fager

Mike Fager is Vice President of Investments and Retirement Specialist with Raymond James and Associates Inc. in Rockford, IL. He has been a Certified Financial Planner (CFP) since 1995. Mike has helped small business owners address the concept of succession planning ever since he started in the financial services industry in 1979. Over the years, he has toured the country and frequently given talks on business-related issues. He is also the designer of a seminar series known as *Lynx for Business*, a program intended to help create networking opportunities for businesses and professionals.

Mike currently focuses on consulting with family business owners and their families on effective transition strategies. It is his firm belief that the key to a successful transition of a family business starts and ends with good family communication.

That last concept is one that he has carried over to his home life. He is the proud father of Justin, Kyle, and Kole and lives in Rockford with his wife, Renee.

Dave McKinney

Dave McKinney is Vice President and Wealth Management Specialist of the Rockford, IL branch of Raymond James & Associates, Inc. He has over 20 years of experience in business and finance, with an extensive background in succession planning. As a Regional Manager for Business Evaluations Systems, he has earned the designations of Senior Business Analyst (SBA) and Certified Machine and Equipment Appraiser (MEA). He is also the President and owner of KLM & Associates, a business brokerage and consulting firm that has coordinated mergers of both publicly and privately owned companies.

Dave first became interested in succession planning when he elected to sell his ownership of DynamicFAX, Inc. (currently called Cleo Software), a privately held communications company. Dave currently dedicates most of his time to consulting to high net worth business owners. He manages their investments as well as offering them comprehensive financial consulting for the life and future of their businesses.

Dave lives in Rockford with his wife Angie and their three children, Kelli, Lindsey, and Michael. He enjoys the outdoors – and even finds time to sneak away to the golf course occasionally.